USN AIR CARRIER AIR UNITS

Volume I
1946-1956

by DUANE A KASULKA

Illustrated by Don Greer

and Kevin Wornkey

squadron/signal publications

COPYRIGHT © 1985
SQUADRON/SIGNAL PUBLICATIONS, INC.
1115 CROWLEY DRIVE, CARROLLTON, TEXAS 75011-5010
All rights reserved. No part of this publication may be reproduced, stored in a retrieval system or transmitted in any form by any means electrical, mechanical or otherwise, without written permission of the publisher.

ISBN 0-89747-164-4

If you have any photographs of the aircraft, armor, soldiers or ships of any nation, particularly wartime snapshots, why not share them with us and help make Squadron/Signal's books all the more interesting and complete in the future. Any photograph sent to us will be copied and the original returned. The donor will be fully credited for any photos used. Please indicate if you wish us not to return the photos. Please send them to: Squadron/Signal Publications, Inc., 1115 Crowley Dr., Carrollton, TX 75011-5010.

DEDICATION:
To my Dad, Alfred E Kasulka who helped construct World War II carriers.

ACKNOWLEDGEMENTS

The author wishes to thank the following individuals and organizations for their assistance in providing photographic and research material. And a special mention regarding the extra effort contributed by the following four individuals.

Roger Besecker   Mike Grove   Bill Larkins   Jim Sullivan

Thank you very much

Jack Anderson	Clay Jansson	Don Spering
Ed Baumann	Larry Kasulka	H Schonenberg
Pete Bowers	Bob Lawson	Gwen Rich
Bob Carlisle	Gerry Margraff	Bill Wagner
Tom Cuddy II	Ernie McDowell	Joe Weathers Jr
Tom Doll	Lional Paul	Gordon Williams
John Durand	Stan Piet Jr	Nick Williams
Bob Esposito	Fred Roos	Jim Wogstad
Harry Gann	Art Schoeni	Don Woods
Grumman Aerospace	McDonnell Douglas	Vought Corp
National Archives	Ryan Aeronautical	United States Navy
North American		

(Above) F4U-1D Corsair of VF-89 at the close of World War II. Carrier Air Group 89 (CVG-89) and its squadrons were decommissioned in April of 1946 as part of the Navy's general demobilization at the end of the Second World War. (Chance Vought)

(Above) SB2C-4E of VB-85 from SHANGRI-LA (CV-38) during August of 1945. The Z on the tail identifies the carrier, while the 82 identifies the aircraft within the carrier air group.

(Below) F9F-2 Panthers of VF-151, flying above WASP (CVA-18) in May of 1955. Many carrier air groups were formed from Navy Air Reserve units activated during the Korean War, becoming Fleet units in 1953. (USN)

USN AIRCRAFT CARRIER AIR UNITS
1946-1956

In the immediate post war years the United States Navy was dominated by problems of demobilization, an uneasy international situation, and a re-organization. Demobilization was rapid with the number of aircraft carriers in service reduced from 109 in 1945 to twenty-five a year later, and by the middle of 1950 to nine. The unsettled international situation in vastly separated areas of the world resulted in the formation of Carrier Task Groups to operate in the North Atlantic, Mediterranean and the Western Pacific, providing tangible evidence of America's presence and support for their Allies and the Free World.

The first of the international crises was quick in coming as President Truman dispatched US Naval forces to Turkey in March of 1946, responding to a massive build-up of Soviet forces along the Turkish border. The next major US foreign policy test came when French, British, and American air forces provided a massive airlift into the city of Berlin, breaking the Soviet surface blockade of the former German capitol.

In some respects this period was almost a repeat of the post World War I twenties. Political clamoring for both a separate air force *and* a merger of all the military services, was satisfied, to a greater or lesser degree, with the creation of the Department of Defense (DOD) in 1947, which combined the three services (the Air Force, Army and Navy) under a single Secretary of Defense. In the Fleet itself, the main problems were the transition to a severely lower force level, the incorporation of World War II combat experience, and the introduction of new weapons and technology. Jet aircraft, guided missiles and nuclear weapons, all required great adjustments in plans, organization and tactic.

The re-organization created by the DOD and the forced agreements among the three services of their respective missions and roles, coupled with a decreasing military budget quickly flared into open dispute as the services fought each other for a larger share of the limited peacetime funds. This increasing interservice fighting had the underlying effect of stifling naval aviation. This became obvious in 1949 when the Secretary of Defense cancelled the Navy's new super aircraft carrier UNITED STATES which had already been funded and agreed to by the President. This high handed cut at naval aviation forced the Navy to fight both the Air Force and the politicians who charged 'duplication', claiming that Navies had become obsolete and that the aircraft carrier was both too vulnerable and too expensive! The result was an ultimatum placed on the Navy by Congress to *develop a nuclear capability without new and larger aircraft carriers or face extinction.* The detonation of a nuclear device by Russia in

HUP-2 Helicopter of HU-2 lifting off FRANKLIN D ROOSEVELT (CVA-42) during August of 1953 to take up station to provide search and rescue (SAR) if required during launch of VC-62 F2H-2P Banshees being positioned at the catapult. (Duane Kasulka Collection)

FR-1 Fireball of VF-1E aboard BADOENG STRAIT (CVE-116) during early 1947 for evaluation of ASW tactics using the Fireball to attack submarine contacts. (Ryan Aeronautical via Bill Wagner)

The Navy's first nuclear bomber, a P2V-3C Neptune of VC-5 being hoisted aboard MIDWAY (CVB-41) during 1948. P2V-3Cs were positioned on the carrier deck and launched with JATO bottles. These nuclear strike aircraft, upon their return from a mission, either landed at a land base or ditched at sea along side the carrier. (USN/NA)

1949 followed by the Korean War, however, brought the Navy's budget problems to a halt as the need for a strong Fleet again became apparent.

With the invasion of South Korea on 25 June 1950 President Truman authorized both Air Force and Navy bombing of Korea, Army support of the Republic of Korea ground forces, and a Naval blockade of the North Korean coasts. Carrier aviation quickly added naval airpower to that of the Air Force when Carrier Air Group Five (CVG -5) off VALLEY FORGE struck targets near the North Korean capitol of Pyongyang on on 3 July. By the end of the month three additional aircraft carriers had arrived off the coast of Korea and naval aviation began carrying the air war to the enemy while the Air Force prepared air fields and brought in aircraft. By the end of the year, eight US aircraft carriers plus a British light carrier would be off the Korean Coasts, and by the end of the war seventeen carriers would see action, several with three tours. During the three years of the Korean War, Navy aircraft flew some 276,000 sorties which was thirty per cent of all sorties flown. Outside of the Korean combat area carrier forces continued to maintain American presence in the Eastern Atlantic and the Mediterranean.

The end of the Korean War on 27 July 1953, did little to decrease world tensions as crisis followed crisis in the Middle East and Far East. The re-emphasis on the *Cold War* gave new importance to the ability of naval carrier aviation of quickly projecting US foreign policy into troubled areas; and the Navy's budget began reflecting a congressional awareness.

The great lesson of the Korean War was that the atomic bomb had not rendered conventional weapons obsolete. It also produced the authorization for a new class of *super aircraft carrier* to replace the World War II ESSEX class carrier. The first of this new class was the FORRESTAL which was authorized in 1951 and commissioned in late 1955. The second, SARATOGA, followed in 1956 at which time there were four additional *super* carriers under construction. This new class of carrier was built specifically for all-weather operation of jet aircraft having nuclear strike capability. The commissioning of these new carriers allowed the Navy to reclassify the ESSEX class carriers, less suited for jet aircraft, as anti-submarine warfare (ASW) carriers and still maintain fifteen of the older attack carriers.

The following covers this eleven year period, the aircraft types, the force levels, the markings, and the color schemes employed by the United States Navy carrier squadrons.

(Above) AD-3 Skyraiders of VA-702 Rustlers, formerly a reserve unit from Dallas, now based aboard BOXER (CV-21), are on there way to bomb targets west of Wonsan, Korea in August of 1951. (USN via Harry Gann)

(Below) AF-2S Guardians of VS-931, a Naval Air Reserve squadron activated during the Korean War, becoming Fleet VS-20 in 1953. The Guardian is launching from BADOENG STRAIT (CVE-116) during August of 1952 off the coast of Korea. (USN)

(Below) Painted in the new scheme of Light Gray over White this FJ-3 Fury of VF-211 is positioned on the forward catapult of BON HOMME RICHARD (CVA-31) during June of 1956. (USN)

CARRIER AIR GROUPS

During the immediate post World War II period carrier Air Groups, were designated according to the type of carrier type: Attack Carrier (CVA), Escort Carrier (CVE), Light Carrier (CVL), and the new Battle Carrier (CVB). The air groups were redesignated by adding a *G* (for Group) suffix letter (with the various air groups now being designated CVAG, CVEG, CVLG, and CVBG). Those Air Groups assigned to night protection of the Fleet also had an *(N)* following the new Air Group designation (Example: CVG(N)-91). All Night Groups were decommissioned by June of 1946, along with several CVEGs. With the postwar demobilization Air Group numbers were out of sequence and difficult to keep track of; on 15 November 1946 the Air Groups were renumbered with their respective Squadrons also being realigned through numerical redesignation.

On 1 September 1948 the CVAGs and CVBGs were redesignated CVGs regardless of their carrier affiliation, with CVLG and CVEG being discontinued as air group designations. These changes are expanded upon in section **Carrier Squadrons** on page 13.

The newly developed anti-submarine warfare (ASW) squadrons continued to operate in groups of two or three squadrons from CVEs until 8 August 1954 when five CVAs were redesignated as Anti-Submarine Warfare aircraft carriers under the designation CVS, while the CVEs were simply decommissioned. The ASW squadrons were not initially established as air groups; this would come later.

Another type of *air group* was the Air Task Group (ATG) which resulted from the difficulty of operating five fighter and attack squadrons plus a variety of special mission composite squadrons from the decks of an ESSEX class carrier under combat conditions. Beginning in January of 1951, the first of what would ultimately become eight Air Task Groups (ATG) was established, two of which saw combat in Korea. Initially to equip these Air Task Groups one squadron from each CVG was temporarily withdrawn to provide them with squadrons.

IDENTIFICATION CODES

POST WAR - Two basic identification systems were employed in the immediate post war period: carrier assigned letter codes and pre-war squadron fuselage codes. There were, of course, variations of both, with some geometric codes also being employed. (Several other identification systems were employed but seemed to to be isolated instances and have been illustrated photographically.) These identification markings were authorized to be a maximum of thirty-six inches high. During this immediate post war period some squadrons used Yellow paint in the application of their identification markings. This came about from the World War Two practice of applying carrier identification markings with washable White, and sometimes Yellow or Medium Green over the High Gloss Dark Blue paint that carrier aircraft began using in mid 1945.

CARRIER ASSIGNED CODES (July 1945) - The system of carrier Air Group identification codes used in the immediate post war period had its origins in a directive issued on 25 July 1945 that assigned a series of *single and double* letter codes to all parent aircraft carriers which were to be displayed on the airplanes of the carrier's assigned air group, replacing the geometric symbols in use at the end of war. The implementation of these new carrier assigned code letters varied and many squadrons continued to use the geometric symbols until the end of the war, and a few geometric symbols lingered on unofficially with some squadrons until early 1947. The exception were the CVE carriers which continued to use geometric symbols on their aircraft until the November of 1946 change. Those aircraft carrying aircraft carrier code letters applied them either on the fuselage or the vertical fin, with aircraft numbers being applied on the fuselage, nose, and/or on the tail section in much smaller digits.

F4U-4 Corsairs of VBF-6 flying over the Pacific at the end of WWII are from HANCOCK (CV-19) and are carrying the carrier's ID code of U on their tails. Aircraft of each squadron is individually numbered starting with 1. (USN)

FR-1 Fireball (39703) of VF-41 at Oakland during October of 1946. The pilot's name, national insignia and tail section are White, while the rear fuselage stripes, trim, and ID codes are in Yellow. These markings seem to be a composite of CVE geometric codes for BAIROKO (CVE-115) combined with the carrier assigned code from SAN JACINTO (CVL-30). This squadron also operated several F6F-5 Hellcats. (Bill Larkins)

TBM-3 Avengers of VT-88 which was decommissioned on 29 October 1945 when CVG-88 was decommissioned. The RR on the tail is the carrier code assigned to YORKTOWN (CV-10). (USN/NA via Fred Roos)

F6F-5 Hellcats of VF-7 carry the M of ENTERPRISE (CV-6) and the aircraft number in Yellow on the fuselage and Yellow on the starboard wing. Seen in February of 1946 while the squadron was based at San Diego. (USN)

SQUADRON ASSIGNED CODES - The pre-World War II fuselage code had been composed of the squadron designater and aircraft number (Example: 18-F-5: squadron 18, fighter, aircraft number 5) which began to appear stateside in 1943 and continued in use in place of the carrier identification letters introduced in July 1945. At least one Air Group applied squadron designators to the vertical fin.

F6F-5 Hellcats of VF-3 stateside after the end of WWII. This squadron was originally VF-6 (1943), the original Shooting Stars. They adopted the Felix emblem when the original Felix squadron was decommissioned. (Cmdr Ed Baumann, USN Ret)

(Left) F8F-1 Bearcat of VF-3, TBM-3E Avenger of VT-3, and a SB2C-5 Helldiver of VB-3 illustrate the useage of squadron designations carried on the fuselage and the air group method of consecutive aircraft numbering. Based on aircraft numbers VBF-3 was not part of CVG-3 during late 1946. (USN via Joe Weathers Jr)

(Below) F8F-1 Bearcats of VBF-20 and VF-20 carrying squadron fuselage codes during 1946. The addition of letters on the top of the tail of these Bearcats are not carrier ID codes but were used as flight ID codes. (Tailhook)

SB2C-4E Helldiver of VT-75 taking off from FRANKLIN D ROOSEVELT (CVB-42) during January of 1946. At this time all CVG-75 squadrons carried this unusual form of indentification on their vertical stablizer. (USN/NA via Tailhook)

F6F-5P (80084) Hellcat of VF-75 with partial markings in 1946. The squadron operated thirty-four F4U-4 Corsair fighters and four photographic Hellcats. The code P3 is the third photographic Hellcat within the squadron. (Gordon Williams Collection)

(Above) This F4U-4 Corsair of VBF-152, over Long Island Sound, carries the high visibility fuselage squadron code used state side. These markings were removed before entering the combat zone. (Jim Sullivan Collection)

F8F-1 of VF-17, this is the 30th Bearcat in the squadron which normally had a strength of twenty-eight to thirty aircraft per squadron. Air Group 17 at this time included VBF-17 (F8Fs), VB-17 (SB2Cs), and VT-17 (TBMs). RCAF Station Rockcliffe during 1946. (via Jim Sullivan)

(Below) SB2C-3E Helldiver of VB-153 over San Francisco in October of 1946. Aircraft within CVG-15 were numbered consecutively. All markings are in White, and the squadron insignia is carried just forward of the cockpit. (Jim Sullivan Collection)

CARRIER ASSIGNED CODES (November 1946) - On 7 November 1946 a directive was issued that updated aircraft carrier identification letters to reflect those carriers in services.

AIRCRAFT NUMBERS (Four Squadron Air Groups) - The same Chief of Naval Operations (CNO) order of 7 November 1946 which updated carrier identification codes, also standardized the system of numbering squadron aircraft by assigning three digit numbers in hundred blocks to each squadron of the then four squadron CVG. The first squadron was assigned numbers beginning with 101, the second squadron with 201, etc. The even hundred numbers (100, 200, etc.) were reserved for the CVG Commander. Prior to this standardization aircraft numbering varied, some squadrons used 1 and up, while others used the hundred series.

F8F-1 Bearcat 0f VF-9A (became VF-191 in 1948) assigned to PHILIP-PINE SEA (CV-47) carrying the newly aligned carrier codes just below the cockpit. (Fred Roos Collection)

F6F-5 (72713) Hellcat of VF-19A flown by Ens Ken Adams during February of 1947. The squadron was previously designated VF-19 'Run In' is chalked on the vertical fin. (Bill Larkins)

F4U-4 of VF-5B (became VF-61 in 1948) is taking off from CORAL SEA (CVB-43) in 1947. The C code was originally assigned to CORAL SEA, in January of 1947 the C code was re-assigned to CVG-5. (USN/NA)

F6F-5 Hellcats of VF-7A carrying CVAG-7 codes on the fuselage that were previously assigned to LEYTE (CV-32). VF-7A is seen operating from the LEYTE near Trinidad during March of 1947. The squadron converted to Bearcats upon completion of this cruise. (USN/NA)

IDENTIFICATION LETTERS

Aircraft Carrier	Code Letters Jul 1945	Code Letters Nov 1946	Air Group Dec 1946
SARATOGA (CV-3)	CC	—	—
RANGER (CV-4)	PP	—	—
ENTERPRISE (CV-6)	M	—	—
ESSEX (CV-9)	F	—	—
YORKTOWN (CV-10)	RR	—	—
INTREPID (CV-11)	E	—	—
HORNET (CV-12)	S	—	—
FRANKLIN (CV-13)	LL	—	—
TICONDEROGA (CV-14)	V		
RANDOLPH (CV-15)	L	R	CVAG-17
LEXINGTON (CV-16)	H	—	—
BUNKER HILL (CV-17)	Y	—	—
WASP (CV-18)	X	—	—
HANCOCK (CV-19)	U	—	—
BENNINGTON (CV-20)	TT	—	—
BOXER (CV-21)	ZZ	B	CVAG-19
INDEPENDENCE (CV-22)	D	—	—
BELLEAU WOOD (CVL-24)	P	—	—
COWPENS (CVL-25)	A	—	—
MONTERACY (CVL-26)	C	—	—
LANGLEY (CVL-27)	K	—	—
CABOT (CVL-28)	R	—	—
BATAAN (CVL-29)	T	—	—
SAN JACINTO (CVL-30)	B	—	—
BON HOMME RICHARD (CV-31)	SS	—	—
LEYTE (CV-32)	—	L	CVAG-7
KEARSARGE (CV-33)	—	K	CVAG-3
ORISKANY (CV-34)	—	RI	CVAG-21
ANTIETAM (CV-36)	W	A	CVAG-15
PRINCETON (CV-37)	—	P	CVAG-13
SHANGRI-LA (CV-38)	Z	S	CVAG-5
LAKE CHAMPLAIN (CV-39)	AA	—	—
TARAWA (CV-40)	—	T	CVAG-1
MIDWAY (CVB-41)	YY	M	CVBG-1
FRANKLIN D ROOSEVELT (CVB-42)	FF	F	CVBG-3
CORAL SEA (CVB-43)	EE	C	CVBG-5
VALLEY FORGE (CV-45)	—	V	CVAG-11
PHILIPPINE SEA (CV-47)	—	PS	CVAG-9
SAIPAN (CVL-48)	—	SA	CVLG-1
WRIGHT (CVL-49)	—	W	—
SALERNO BAY (CVE-110)	—	SB	—
SIBONEY (CVE-112)	—	SI	—
RENDOVA (CVE-114)	—	RE	—
BAIROKO (CVE-115)	—	BA	—
BADOENG STRAIT (CVE-116)	—	BS	CVEG-1
SALDOR (CVE-117)	—	SR	—
SICILY (CVE-118)	—	SL	CVEG-2
POINT CRUZ (CVE-119)	—	PZ	—
MINDORO (CVE-120)	—	MI	CVEG-3
PALAU (CVE-122)	—	PA	

Note: *Not all identification letters were used. Some carrier air groups continued the use of geometric codes, and other air groups were not in service as a result of battle damage, or hud not yet been commissioned, while others were involved in OPERATION MAGIC CARPET which transported US servicemen home in late 1945 and early 1946.*

AIR GROUP ASSIGNED CODES (December 1946) - A month, later on 12 December 1946, the identification letters were assigned to the carrier air groups (CVGs) rather than to the aircraft carriers, and standards of applying these new identification letters was defined. The location of CVG identification letters was ordered to be displayed on both sides of the vertical fin and rudder, and on the upper starboard wing and lower port wing near the tips, effective 2 January 1947. These code letters were the beginning of what was to become known as *tail codes*, which were now assigned to the carrier air groups, regardless of which aircraft carrier the air group was assigned, or which squadrons were assigned to the air group.

NATIONAL INSIGNIA - A few weeks later, on 14 January 1947, a mandatory change brought the National Insignia to its present composition, with the addition of a Red stripe centered on the White horizontal bar.

(Above) F8F-1 (95318) Bearcat of VF-20A (became VF-192 in 1948), the second fighter squadron within CVAG-19 flying over San Francisco in June of 1947. (Bill Larkins)

(Left) F4U-4 Corsair of VF-5B (became VF-61 in 1948) carrying the tail code C of CVG-6 on the vertical stabelizer and lower port wing tip, only the squadron aircraft number 116 is carried on the fuselage.(USN/NA via Jim Sullivan)

(Above) F8F-1 (94786) Bearcat of VF-1L as part of CVLG-1 at Altantic City just before being decommissioned on 4 August 1948. (Roger Besecker Collection)

(Below) TBM-3E Avenger of VA-16A (became VA-155 in 1948) as part of CVAG-15 prepares for for takeoff at Alameda in 1948. (Tailhook)

AD-1 (09162) Skyraider of VA-3B during May of 1947, just one month after receiving their new Skyraiders in April of 1947. With the squadron redesignation of 1948, VA-3B became VA-44 and changed their aircraft numbers to a 400 series. (Roger Besecker)

9

TRIM COLORS - With the establishment of a CVG identification system individual squadron trim color coding followed on 1 May 1948. Prior to this some squadrons had adopted their own choice of trim colors and trim location. These newly assigned colors were directed to be applied to the spinner and the top seven inches of the vertical fin and rudder. However, in practice squadron trim colors appeared in a variety of locations including wing tips and nose cowls; more at the dictates of squadron COs than the 1948 directive. Jet aircraft initially did not carry squadron trim colors on the nose, many squadrons equipped with jets devised color schemes incorporating trim colors on wing tips or wingtip fuel tanks and fuselage bands. It would be near the end of the Korean War before extensive use of color began to appear on Navy aircraft. The 1948 directive also changed the location and increased the size of the aircraft designator, bureau number, and the service marking *NAVY*. The aircraft designator was moved from the fin, being relocated below the leading edge of the horizontal tailplane. The service marking (*NAVY*) was increased in size to two inches, while the bureau number was increased to four inches in height.

AIRCRAFT NUMBERS (Nine Squadron Air Groups) - On 4 August 1948 a directive expanded the three digit aircraft numbers to include up to nine squadrons within an air group and modified the Air Group Commander (CAG) aircraft numbering system. The hundred series were to be used as follows: the first digit, 1 through 6, indicated the squadron within the CVG and the last two numbers indicated the aircraft within the squadron. The squadron designators were now aligned to match the parent CVG. The squadron aircraft number by this time was carried inboard of the tail code on the upper right and lower left wing tips. The aircraft number was usually about 3/4 of the height of the tail code and was applied in the same color. Numbers applied to a composite squadron had usually started with 1, but after this change some DETs in the 1950s began to use the hundred series numbers when deployed with an air group.

F4U-5 Corsair of VF-21 aboard CORAL SEA (CVB-43) during June of 1949. Standard trim color for a 100 series squadron aircraft was Red, but VF-21 used White. (USN/NA via Jim Sullivan)

F4U-5NL Corsairs of VC-3, part of a night fighter DET aboard ANTIETAM (CVS-36) to provide carrier air defense. Note the application of a 600 series squadron aircraft number. (Chance Vought)

F8F-2 (121546) Bearcat of VF-72 with White tail trim as directed for the second squadron within a CVG. VF-72 deployed to the Mediterranean aboard MIDWAY (CVB-42) during the summer of 1950. (Bob Esposito Collection)

AD-1 (123835) Skyraider of VA-115 carrying Green trim of the fifth sqaudron per the May of 1948 directive. All other markings are in White. (USN)

AD-4W Skyraider of VC-12, DET 38 aboard WASP (CVA-18) during 1952. Composite squadrons on the East Coast quickly began using the newly assigned hundred series squadron numbers while those squadrons on the West Coast continued to use 1 or 2 diget numbers. (Ernie McDowell)

F2H-2P (128857) Banshee of VC-61 during July of 1953 carrying the new 900 aircraft numbers for photo DETS. (USN)

HIGH VISIBILITY MARKINGS - On 12 May 1950 *high visibility markings* were adopted, increasing the size of the service marking *NAVY* to at least twelve inches high and moving it to the rear fuselage just forward of the horizontal stabilizer, with the squadron designater being added just below the service marking. By this time the National Insignia on many jet aircraft was being applied to each side of the nose instead of the rear fuselage. The service markings were painted outboard on the lower port wing surface replacing the air group code, however the aircraft number was temporarily retained on both the lower port and upper starboard wing. The CVG tail code that had been carried on the lower port wing tip was moved to the under surface of the starboard wing midway between the National Insignia and the fuselage. The aircraft number on the lower left wing was reduced in size and moved in-board. Authorization was given to paint the full squadron designater under the word *NAVY* in White eight inch high letters on both sides of the rear fuselage. The letter *V*, formerly used for administration only, was now in-cluded in the squadron designater.

Another type of high visibility markings were temporarily used on aircraft involved in war training exercises. Large bands of washable White paint were added to the wings and fuselage. And while unofficial, these White bands were used to distinguish aircraft of the opposing force.

These AD-4Q (124047) Skyraiders of VA-55 illustrate the transitions that introduced high visibility markings. On the aircraft in the background the lower wing has had the aircraft number and tail code replaced with the service name, while aft fuselage changes include the size and location of the national insignia and the addition of the service marking. (USN)

F4U-5NL Corsair of VC-3 being towed forward aboard BOXER (CVA-21) during May of 1952. Mission markings and nickname are visible in front of the cockpit. (USN)

FJ-3 (135978) Fury of VF-154 at Moffett Field in May of 1956, decked out in trim colors of Yellow outlined in White. (Bill Larkins)

This F2H-2 Banshee of VF-172, recovering aboard ESSEX (CVA-9) in 1952 off the coast of Korea, illustrates the relocation of the star and bar to the nose of jet aircraft. Note the change in under wing mark-ings adopted in 1950. (USN via Fred Roos)

F9F-5 Panther aboard BOXER (CV-21) during February of 1953 carry-ing Commander Air Group 11 (CAG-11) markings which include the 00 nose number, the multi-colored nose rings of Red, White and the Dark Gloss Blue of the aircraft, and the CAG insignia under the canopy. The aircraft belongs to VF-113 as noted by the insignia next to the CAG insignia. (USN/NA via Jim Sullivan)

Swept wing F9F-6 Cougars of VF-191 carrying CVG-19 tail codes that are partially obscured by the special White markings that designate these aircraft as part of the opposing force during training exercices. The Cougars are awaiting launch from ORISKANY (CVA-34) in March of 1954. (USN)

KOREAN WAR MARKINGS

With the outbreak of the Korean War all lettering on night fighters, was changed from White to less visible Non-Specular Red. When these precautions proved unnecessary all night fighter lettering was repainted in White. During the Korean conflict individual aircraft color schemes began to reappear. Squadrons were permitted to decorate their aircraft with splashes of Red and White on the noses of jet aircraft and the cowls of propeller driven aircraft. Marine Corps squadrons seem to have led the way and special identifying color schemes began to appear on their aircraft. As they did World War II, the Navy again permitted miniature flags, silhouettes of enemy aircraft, ships, and bombs to signify victories. However, unlike the Air Force, the Navy suppressed the use of individual aircraft names, decorations, and insignias on their aircraft.

Another type of markings that appeared during the Korean war were applied to an aircraft when its pilot landed on the wrong carrier. These unofficial markings were usually applied in washable paint and resembled graffiti more than anything else! With the unfortunate pilot having to fly back to his own carrier and wash the graffiti off of his aircraft.

AD-3Q (122871) Skyraider of VA-35 aboard MIDWAY (CVB-41) prepares to launch in August of 1952. Commander Air Group (CAG) aircraft numbers were 00 to 99 during this time period. Squadron trim colors are carried on the tip of the vertical fin. The CAG's first name was Hank, and this was his retirement flight. (D Walsh via Bill Larkins)

F4U-5 (121870) Corsair of VF-44 departing MIDWAY (CVB-41) in November of 1951 loaded with grafitti. Pilots who landed aboard the wrong carrier during the Korean War suffered this fate and the pilot later paid the price when he had to wash it off. (USN/NA via Jim Sullivan)

(Below) F2H-2 (125019) Banshee of VF-62 from CORAL SEA (CVA-43) in 1953 after landing aboard WASP (CVA-18). This was all done in fun during the Korean War but the poor pilot had to return with his new markings to the ribbing of his air group. (Ernie McDowell)

(Above) F9F-2B Panther of VF-111 carries out yet another strike in Korea during 1952. This aircraft already has over 115 missions painted on the fuselage as silhoueted bombs in groups of five. (USN)

F4U-4 (81079) Corsair of VF-713 from ANTIETAM (CVA-36) over the Korean Coast in January of 1952. Mission marks are carried just below the windscreen. (USN/NA via Jim Sullivan)

KOREAN WAR RESERVE CALL UP AND RE-DESIGNATIONS

During the Korean War the Navy recalled two reserve CVGs and re-commissioned two reserve CVGs as Fleet CVGs. Each of these CVGs were formed with four fighter-bomber squadrons of F4U Corsairs or F8F Bearcats, and one AD Skyraider squadron. During 1953 the two reserve CVGs and all 20 reserve squadrons activated during the Korean War were re-designated as Fleet units.

CVG-8		"E"	CVG-15		"H"
Reserve Station			**Reserve Station**		
Atlanta	VF-671	to VF-81	Akron	VF-653	to VF-151
Jacksonville	VF-742	to VF-82	Denver	VF-713	to VF-152
Squantum	VF-916	to VF-83	New York	VF-831	to VF-153
St Louis	VF-921	to VF-84	New York	VF-837	to VF-154
Niagara Falls	VA-859	to VA-85	Glenview	VA-728	to VA-155
CVG-102 to CVG-12		"D"	**CVG-101 to CVG-14**		"A"
Reserve Station			**Reserve Station**		
Los Alamitos	VF-781	to VF-121	Glenview	VF-721	to VF-141
Los Alamitos	VF-783	to VF-122	Memphis	VF-791	to VF-142
Oakland	VF-871*	to VF-123	New Orleans	VF-821*	to VF-143
Oakland	VF-874	to VF-124	Olathe	VF-884	to VF-144
St Louis	VA-923	to VA-125	Dallas	VA-702	to VA-145

*CVG-8 and CVG-15 were recommissioned in April of 1951 (squadrons in Feb). CVG-101 and CVG-102 were re-called in August of 1950 (squadrons in Jul). *Initially assigned to CVG-19.*

NEW AIR GROUPS - The Navy had only nine Carrier Air Groups (CVGs) when the Korean War brokeout, down from fifteen only two years before. In need of a quick increase in force Naval Reserves were called up to form two Reserve CVGs and two re-commissioned Fleet CVGs. The re-commissioning of other CVGs activated prior tail codes, and in several cases new tail codes had to be issued since their original tail codes were sometimes in use by new CVGs.

Assignment of squadrons from one CVG to another resulted in some squadrons retaining their prior CVG tail codes. This was especially noticeable when squadrons were assigned to Air Task Groups (ATGs). The ATGs were *unofficial* air groups with squadrons assigned to them from various CVGs, and may account for the retention of the parent CVG tail code being retained on aircraft rather than applying the tail codes of the ATG to which they were assigned. By the end of the Korean War there were sixteen CVGs and two ATGs. The end of hostilities in Korea did not reduce world tension and the Navy continued to build up its forces so that by 1956 there were seventeen CVGs, and eight ATGs supported by 102 fighter and attack squadrons plus twenty composite squadrons. Near the end of this time period ATG tail codes began to appear, but not on all squadrons.

This F2H-4 (127654) of VF-11 illustrates the colorfulness of the markings that came into vogue during the mid 50s. This Red Ripper Banshee carries a squadron insignia, Red and White lighting bolts, White trim, and White markings. (MDAC via Fred Harl)

(Below) F9F-8 (131138) Cougar of VF-13 attached to Air Task Group 201 (ATG-201). The ᴀᴛɢ tail code cleverly contains the T tail code of CVG-1 from which the Panthers have been assigned, with the ᴀᴛɢ combination standing for Air Task Group. Trim is Light Blue with White Stars and outline. (Harry Gann)

CARRIER AIR GROUP/AIR TASK GROUP LINEAGE
TYPE OF IDENTIFICATION LETTER ASSIGNMENT

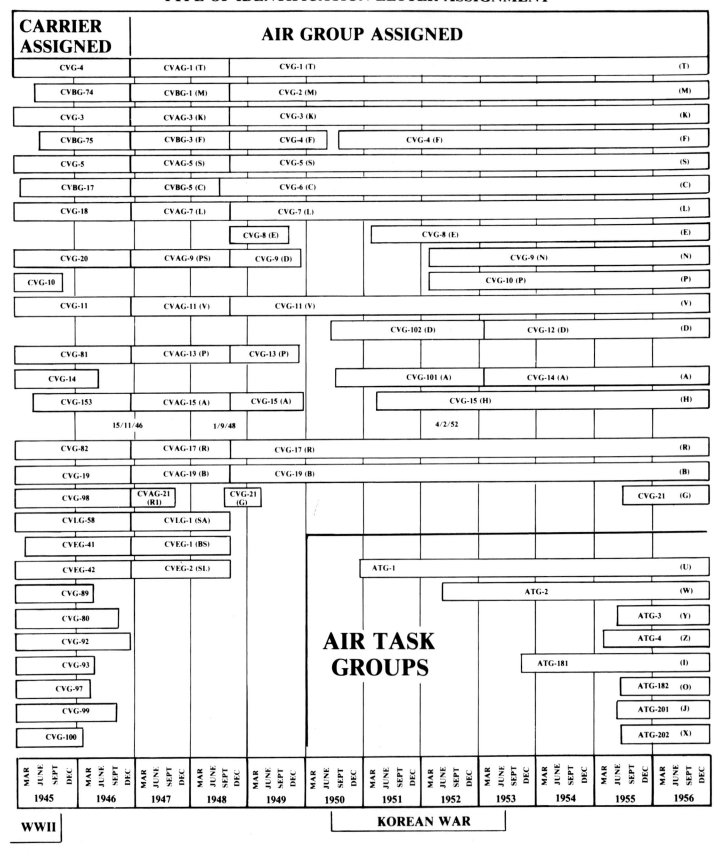

NEW AIRCRAFT COLORS

Korean War experience had shown that the overall Gloss Dark Blue finish was too conspicuous at high altitudes. In 1953 tests were conducted with experimental aircraft color schemes. As a result of these tests Navy and Marine Corps squadrons began receiving aircraft in bare metal finish during 1954, however bare metal aircraft proved extremely difficult to maintain in the saltwater environment in which the Navy and Marine Corps usually operated. The color scheme eventually selected for service use was Matt Gull Gray applied to the top and sides of the aircraft over Gloss White undersurfaces. This new Light Gray over White scheme was introduced in February of 1955, with carrier aircraft delivered after 1 July 1956 to be in compliance with the new scheme and those in service conforming within a year. The results were that most squadrons operated a mixture of both schemes for a while.

NEW TRIM COLORS - Trim colors were revised on 9 March 1955 to reflect the new Light Gray over White color scheme.

Old Trim Color	New Trim Color
White	Orange-Yellow
Light Yellow	International Orange
Black outlined in White	Black

Maroon was added for additional squadrons and detachments (DETs). The special block of aircraft numbers reserved for the Air Group Commander (CAG) was officially discontinued and the use of even hundred numbers for squadron aircraft was resumed. These new trim colors were basically an official acceptance of what had been in use since the early 1950s. Multi-colors were allocated for the CAG's aircraft composed of the various squadron trim colors. With the 9 March 1955 change the lower port wing had all markings removed, leaving only the national insignia on the starboard wing being visible from below.

SQUADRON AIRCRAFT NUMBERS AND TRIM COLORS

Command	Nov 1946	May 1948	Aug 1948	Mar 1955
CAG	X00 Series	—	0 to 99	X00
1st Sqdn	101 and up	Insignia Red	101 and up	Insignia Red
2nd Sqdn	201 and up	Insignia White	201 and up	Orange-Yellow
3rd Sqdn	301 and up	Light Blue	301 and up	Light Blue
4th Sqdn	401 and up	Light Yellow	401 and up	International-Orange
5th Sqdn	—	Light Green	501 and up	Light Green
6th Sqdn	—	Black outlined in White	601 and up	Black
7th Sqdn	—	—	701 and up	Maroon
8th Sqdn	—	—	801 and up	—
9th Sqdn	—	—	901 and up	—

FJ-3 (149247) Furies of VF-33 in natural metal are flying above El Centro in early 1957. Unpainted natural metal was found to be difficult to maintain and was replaced by the Light Gray over White paint scheme. (USN/NA via Jim Sullivan)

(Left) F9F-5 (126657) Panther of VF-153 illustrates the mixture of aircraft color schemes during the camouflage evaluation of the mid '50s. Two battle damaged aircraft, one in natural metal, the other in Gloss Dark Blue, have been salvaged to create one flyable aircraft. (USN/NA via Jim Sullivan)

(Above) F9F-5 (125634) Panther of VF-192 at San Francisco in August of 1954 in the rarely seen Aluminum paint scheme. Wording under the horizontal stabilizer reads: THIS IS AN EXPERIMENTAL FINISH DO NOT PAINT WITHOUT SPECIFIC AUTHORIZATION, SEE LOG BOOK. (Bill Larkins)

(Above) F3H-2N (133635) Demon of VF-61 aboard RANGER (CVA-61) during late 1956. The removal of the tail code and aircraft number from the lower left wing was mandated in March of 1955. (MDAC via Fred Harl)

(Below) F2H-2 Banshees of VC-4 carrying CVG-17's R tail code and the new 600 series aircraft numbers assigned to all-weather fighter units, flying past Mount Fuji in September of 1954. VC-4's squadron code of NA is carried on the Red trimmed fin cap. (MDAC via Fred Roos)

15

CARRIER AIRGROUP COMMANDER (CAG)

F4U-5 (121846) Corsair in CAG-1 markings. The double digit method of numbering CAG aircraft was introduced in 1948, but was usually ignored with the preferred hundred series system remaining in general use. Cherry Point 1950. (Jim Sullivan Collection)

F6F-5 Hellcat of VF-3, designated Commander Air Group Three: CDR L M BAUER CAG3. The Navy used a V for air, so carrier air groups were designated as CVGs, but the Commander of the air group were referred to as CAG! (USN via Joe Weathers, Jr)

(Above) F8F-2 (121701) Bearcat of CVG-15 from ANTIETAM (CV-36). The 0 indicates that this is the CAG's aircraft, which is trimmed with Red and White over the aircrafts Glossy Dark Blue finish, October of 1949. This single digit CAG numbering system, introduced in September of 1948, only lasted a short time. (Bill Larkins)

(Below) AD-5 (133912) designated as the CAG of Air Task Group Three (ATG-3)! The Skyraiders of ATG-3 were operated by VF-192 from Miramar in 1956. This Skyraider equipped squadron deployed aboard SHANGRI-LA (CVA-38) in January of 1956 for a six month cruise equipped with AD-4Bs and AD-4NAs. This AD-5 was for shore based utility duties. VF-192 converted to F2H Banshees after this cruise. (Bill Larkins Collection)

F8F-1 (95320) Bearcat flown by Cmdr.H.E.Cook Jr., of CAG-19, at Alameda during June of 1947 carrying the new hundred series (00) CAG ID numbers, which were officially sanctioned in 1946. (Bill Larkins)

FJ-3 (136155) Fury of VF-24 in carrier air group (CVG) colors with a multi-color rudder which became common place after the introduction of the Light Gray over White color scheme. (Pete Bowers via Jim Sullivan)

(Above) AD-5 (132646) Skyraider belonging to VA-216, the sixth squadron in the newly commissioned CVG-21 on July of 1956. This CAG aircraft has its squadron trim colors in Red diamonds on a field of White. (Bill Larkins Collection)

(Below) A4D-1 (149522) Skyhawk of VA-72 launching from RANDOLPH (CVA-15) in late 1956. The useage of 'double nuts' (00) was normally carried on an aircraft from the squadron that the CAG orginally flew with. (MDAC via Harry Gann)

COMPOSITE SQUADRONS - Composite squadrons (VCs), introduced in 1948, carried their own individual double letter tail codes and retained these even while attached to a CVG. However, this began to change in 1952 when carrier air group's tail codes began to replace squadrons codes. This was especially true of CVGs assigned to the larger carriers, and it would seem that the decision was at the discretion of the air group commander (CAG).

(Above) F9F-6 (127307) Cougar of VC-4 taking off from Altantic City in May of 1955. Only a few Cougars were used by VC-4 for flight proficiency. (USN/NA via Jim Sullivan)

(Above) F2H-3 (127511) Banshee of VC-3 equipped with a refueling probe at Moffett Field in May of 1955. The aircraft number suggests that they are part of a fighter DET aboard a CVS carrier to provide air protection. (Bill Larkins)

(Below) F2H-2P (125684) Banshee of VC-62 aboard FRANKLIN D ROOSEVELT (CVA-42) in Nineth Squadron aircraft numbers during the summer of 1953. (USN via Jim Sullivan)

MARINE CORPS SQUADRONS - Marine Corps squadrons operating from escort carriers (CVEs) during the post war period, underlined their carrier codes in White to illustrate that they were USMC units. With the 7 November 1946 directive assigning new air group codes, USMC squadrons were assigned the CVE codes from which they were operating, while other Marine squadrons carried individually assigned squadron tail codes. These changes eliminated the need for the White underline, though the underline continued in use for some time. As CVEs were phased out of service, USMC squadrons were assigned to CVGs where they continued to use their own assigned tail codes and hundred series aircraft numbers. By the late 1950s Marine CVG codes were beginning to be used.

(Below) F4U-4 (81945) Corsair of VMF-214 based aboard RENDOVA (CVE-114), in August of 1947. Marine Corps squadrons operating from CVEs during this time period carried a White bar under the carrier code. (Clay Jansson)

FJ-3 Fury of VMF-122 aboard CORAL SEA (CVA-43), is attached to CVG-3 during the 1955 cruise. USMC squadrons were frequently assigned to CVGs when Navy squadrons were unavailable during their transitioning to a new aircraft. (USMC)

On **15 November 1956** there was a Fleet wide change of tail codes with a new series of CVG tail codes composed of double letters. The Composite squadrons, which were redesignated in July to align their designations with their roles, also received a new series of double letter tail codes. Those squadron aircraft marked with the old codes remained until the aircraft went through maintenance, or until mid-1957 when all tail codes were to be in conformance with the 1956 directive. These new tail codes will be covered in volume II.

CARRIER SQUADRONS

At the end of World War II most carrier air groups (CVGs) were composed of a fighter squadron (VF), a fighter-bomber squadron (VBF), a bomber squadron (VB), and a torpedo squadron (VT). With the 15 November 1946 re-alignment of Carrier Air Groups and the associated re-designation which placed aircraft carrier type suffix letters after the squadron designator to distinguish between squadrons of the same designation but assigned to a different aircraft carrier class (CVA, CVE, etc.). The results were that VF squadrons used the group number, VB squadrons were redesignated as attack squadrons (VAs) and used the group number, while VBF and VT squadrons were redesignated VF and VA respectively and used the next even number greater than the group number. This new designation system was exceedingly complex and caused considerable confusion. This was soon apparent, and effective 1 September 1948 a new system was implemented that redesignated and re-aligned squadrons according to their air groups, and at the same time the CVGs were restructured with the addition of a third fighter squadron with each squadron having eighteen to twenty aircraft. The re-designated attack squadrons (VAs) remained near their World War II complement of sixteen to eighteen torpedo and bomber aircraft. The multi-seat World War II aircraft began being replaced by new single seat medium attack bombers in 1946. The introduction of the jet fighter into the Fleet during 1948 spelled the end of propeller driven interceptors, but the fighter-bomber role remained with the propeller driven World War II airplanes since the initial jet aircraft lacked heavy bombload carrying capability.

Another change in the composition of the CVG was the introduction of specialized aircraft during 1948, which were consolidated into *COMPOSITE SQUADRONS* with dedicated missions providing specialized detachments (DETs) to an air group. This new type of squadron continued to increase in numbers and by 1951 there were nine such composite squadrons in service. A carrier air group (CVG) now included five squadrons; two jet interceptor/strike escort squadrons (VFs), two propeller driven fighter-bomber squadrons (VBFs), and a medium attack-bomber squadron. Composite squadrons normally operated as detachments (DETs) from their parent squadrons with one to five aircraft being assigned to a CVG, dependent upon aircraft type, carrier size and mission. Typically these included a DET of night-fighters, night/counter-measure attack, photographic, early warning, heavy attack, and helicopter utility for Search and Rescue (SAR). On 15 July 1956 those squadrons still designated as composite detachments were redesignated by their prime role, VF(AW), VA(AW), VFP, VAW, VAH and HU.

By 1954 those air groups assigned to escort class carriers (CVEs) that had converted to jet operations had been assigned five squadrons. The composition of the CVE assigned carrier air groups began to evolve into one fighter interceptor squadron, one all-weather fighter squadron, two light attack fighter-bomber squadrons, and a fifth squadron of medium attack bombers. CVGs aboard MIDWAY class carriers added a sixth squadron, consisting of either another jet fighter squadron or a second medium attack squadron. In addition a heavy attack composite squadron was added. Both classes of aircraft carrier operated a standard mix of special mission composite squadrons. Full all-weather fighter squadrons began replacing the composite squadron night-fighter DETs except on the smaller carriers. By the close of this time period the emphasis of carrier air groups had slowly shifted from the fighter role to the attack role. Air Task Groups (ATGs) had similar squadron mixes, but with their squadrons temporarily being assigned to them from a variety of CVGs.

Expanded anti-submarine warfare (ASW) units operated initially aboard CVEs, and beginning in 1954 began operating aboard CVAs that were not able to handle jet aircraft. These CVAs were converted to the ASW role and redesignated to CVSs. ASW units had evolved into a fixed wing anti-submarine squadron, a helicopter anti-submarine squadron, and a DET from an early warning squadron. When an anti-submarine aircraft carrier (CVS) operated in a Task Force (TF) without the support of an attack carrier (CVA), a DET from a fighter squadron was added for combat air patrol (CAP).

CARRIER AIR GROUP AND SQUADRON RE-DESIGNATIONS

Post War	15 Nov 1946	1 Sept 1948	Post War	15 Nov 1946	1 Sept 1948	Post War	15 Nov 1946	1 Sept 1948
CVG-4	CVAG-1	CVG-1	CVBG-74	CVBG-1	CVG-2	CVG-3	CVAG-3	CVG-3
VF-4	VF-1A	VF-11	VF-74	VF-1B	VF-21	VF-3	VF-3A	VF-31
VBF-4	VF-2A	VF-12	VBF-74	VF-2B	VF-22	VBF-3	VF-4A	VF-32
—	—	VF-13	—	—	VF-23	—	—	VF-33
VB-4	VA-1A	VA-14	VB-74	VA-1B	VA-24	VB-3	VA-3A	VA-34
VT-4	VA-2A	VA-15	VT-74	VA-2B	VA-25	VT-3	VA-4A	VA-35
CVBG-75	CVBG-3	CVG-4	CVG-5	CVAG-5	CVG-5	CVBG-17	CVBG-5	CVG-6
VF-75	VF-3B	VF-41	VF-5	VF-5A	VF-51	VF-17	VF-5B	VF-61
VBF-75	VF-4B	VF-42	VBF-5	VF-6A	VF-52	VBF-17	VF-6B	VF-62
—	—	VF-43	—	—	VF-53	—	—	VF-63
VB-75	VA-3B	VA-44	VB-5	VA-5A	VA-54	VB-17	VB-5B	VA-64
VT-75	VA-4B	VA-45	VT-5	VA-6A	VA-55	VT-17	VB-6B	VA-65
CVG-18	CVAG-7	CVG-7	CVG-20	CVAG-9	CVG-9	CVAG-11	CVAG-11	CVG-11
VF-18	VF-7A	VF-71	VF-20	VF-9A	VF-91	VF-11	VF-11A	VF-111
VBF-18	VF-8A	VF-72	VBF-20	VF-10A	VF-92	VBF-11	VF-12A	VF-112
—	—	VF-73	—	—	VF-93	—	—	VF-113
VB-18	VA-7A	VA-74	VB-20	VA-9A	VA-94	VB-11	VA-11A	VA-114
VT-18	VA-8A	VA-75	VT-20	VA-10A	VA-95	VT-11	VA-12A	VA-115
CVG-81	CVAG-13	CVG-13	CVG-15	CVAG-15	CVG-15	CVG-82	CVAG-17	CVG-17
VF-81	VF-13A	VF-131	VF-15	VF-15A	VF-151	VF-82	VF-17A	VF-171
VBF-81	VF-14A	VF-132	VBF-15	VF-16A	VF-152	VBF-82	VF-18A	VF-172
—	—	VF-133	—	—	VF-153	—	—	VF-173
VB-81	VA-13A	VA-134	VB-15	VA-15A	VA-154	VB-82	VA-17A	VA-174
VT-81	VA-14A	VA-135	VT-15	VA-16A	VA-155	VT-82	VA-18A	VA-175
CVG-19	CVAG-19	CVG-19	CVG-98	CVAG-21	CVG-21*	CVLG-58	CVLG-1	VX-3**
VF-19	VF-19A	VF-191	VF-98	VF-21A	VF-211	VF-58	VF-1L	Decom
VBF-19	VF-20A	VF-192	VBF-98	VF-22A	VF-212	VT-58	VA-1L	Decom
—	—	VF-193	—	—	VF-213	—	—	—
VB-19	VA-19A	VA-194	VB-98	VA-21A	VA-214	—	—	—
VT-19	VA-20A	VA-195	VT-98	VA-22A	VA-215	—	—	—
CVEG-41	CVEG-1	CV-21	CVEG-42	CVEG-2	VC-22	CVEG-43	CVEG-3	VC-23
VF-41	VF-1E	Decom	VF-42	VF-2E	Decom	VF-43	VF-3E	Decom
VT-41	VA-1E	Decom	VT-42	VA-2E	Decom	VT-43	VA-3E	Decom

* CVAG-21 decommissioned 5 Sept 1947, CVG-21 commissioned 15 Sept 1948.
** Squadrons merged into VX-3 on 4 August 1948.

FIGHTER AND ATTACK AIRCRAFT

Both post war fighter squadrons (VFs) and fighter-bomber squadrons (VBFs) normally operated the same type of aircraft within a given air group. Fighter types included the Grumman F6F Hellcat, Chance Vought F4U Corsair, Grumman F8F Bearcat and the Ryan FR Fireball.

TBM AVENGER and SB2C HELLDIVER - The bomber squadrons (VBs) operated Curtiss SB2C-5, -4E and licensed built Canadian Car and Foundry built SBW-4E Helldivers, alongside torpedo squadrons (VTs) operating Grumman TBM-3, -3E, -3W, -3Q Avengers and SB2C-4E, -5 Helldivers. The Avenger lingered on until 1949 when only three squadrons remained with the now re-designated attack squadron (VA) community, and the Helldivers were gone by mid-year. Both types being replaced initially by Douglas AD Skyraiders, and later also by Martin AM Maulers.

(Above) TBM-3E (53576) Avenger of VA-35 being hoisted aboard LEYTE (CV-32) as part of CVG-3 at Quonset Point in April of 1949. (Tailhook)

(Left) TBM-3E Avengers of VT-83 off ESSEX (CV-9) flying over the coast of Japan at the end of World War II. A month later, along with the other squadrons of CVG-83, VT-83 was decommissioned. (USN)

(Above) TBM-3E Avengers of VA-18A in July of 1948. VA-18A would be re-designated VA-175 two months later with its aircraft receiving 500 series numbers. (Tailhook)

(Below) SB2C-4E (65254) Helldiver of VB-20 in July of 1946, the squadron was redesignated VA-9A in November of 1946, and again re-designated to VA-94 in September of 1948. (Pete Bowers Collection)

(Above) SB2C-4E of VT-75 stateside during 1946. While the use of the squadron designator on the vertical fin was extremely rare, the application of VT on the wing was only known to have been used by the squadrons of CVBG-75. Normally the designator on the wing would be 75-T-2. (Bill Larkins Collection)

(Below) SB2C-5 Helldivers of VB-87 from TICONDEROGA (CV-14) returning from their last strike on Japan. These aircraft carrier tail codes remained in effect until November of 1946 when Air Group codes were established. (USN)

(Below) SB2C-5 Helldiver of VB-5B (became VA-64 in 1948) at the Cleveland National Air Races in August of 1947. They had previously been assigned to CORAL SEA (CVB-42), and still carry the C tail code of Coral Sea which was assigned in 1946. (Pete Bowers Collection)

(Below) SB2C-4 (83631) Helldiver of VA-13A (became VA-134 during 1948) aboard BOXER (CV-21) in 1947. (Pete Bowers Collection)

F6F HELLCAT - Fighter squadrons in the immediate post war years performed secondary roles by operating photo reconnaissance aircraft (F6F-5P), and radar adapted Hellcats for night protection of the Fleet (F6F-5E/-5N). Beginning in 1949 these secondary roles would be carried out by detachments (DETs) of the newly commissioned composite squadrons (VCs). By 1948 the F6F Hellcat was gone, being replaced by the F4U Corsair and the newer F8F Bearcat, both of which remained in post-war production.

(Above) F6F-5 Hellcats of VF-8 aboard RANDOLPH (CV-15) at the close of World War II carrying RANDOLPH's code letter L on their tails. CVG-8 was de-commissioned on 23 November 1945 but was re-commissioned three years later and assigned the tail code letter E. (USN)

(Above) F6F-5 Hellcat of VBF-20 carrying the squadron designator on the fuselage denoting that this is also the CO's aircraft. Typically the CO's aircraft was noted with the numeral one (example: 20-VBF-1). (Bill Larkins Collection)

(Below) F6F-5P Hellcat of VF-9A (became VF-91 in 1948) that came to grief during mid 1947. VF-9A operated twenty-five F8F-1 Bearcats and two F6F-5P photographic Hellcats. (Fred Roos Collection)

(Below) F6F-5P Hellcat of VF-5B (became VF-61 in 1948) during March of 1948 aboard CORAL SEA (CVB-43). The squadron operated F4U-4 Corsairs along with several Hellcats for photo duties. (Tailhook)

(Below) F6F-5 (78264) Hellcat of VF-11A during 1948 when the squadron operated twenty-one F8F-1 Bearcats, one F6F-5 Hellcat, and one F6F-5P Hellcat. The aircraft numeral 1 would imply that this is the CAG's aircraft. (E Galbraith via Tailhook)

F4U CORSAIR - The F4U Corsair, like the Bearcat, was considered obsolete, but remained in fleet service in the fighter-bomber role. With the outbreak of the Korean War the Navy redesignated one attack squadron from each carrier air group to a fighter squadron, raising the total to four fighter squadrons since insufficient AD Skyraider attack aircraft were available. The majority of these redesignated fighter squadrons were initially equipped with the F4U Corsairs which peaked at a total of twenty-eight squadrons in 1952, and which were equipped with the F4U-4, F4U-4B, F4U-5, and the Goodyear license built FG-1D. The F4U-4B and -5 Corsairs had provisions for two 1000 pound bomb racks and eight pylons for rockets. In early 1954 VF-74 was the last operational full Corsair fighter squadron.

(Above) F4U-4 Corsair of VF-3B (became VF-41 in 1948) with CVBG-3, the F code was originally assigned to the FRANKLIN D ROOSEVELT (CVB-42). (Bob Esposito)

(Left) F4U-4 (81616) Corsair of VBF-74 with a liberal application of Yellow trim color on the vertical fin during 1946. This was prior to the issuance of official trim colors. (Via Jim Sullivan)

(Above) F4U-4B of VA-74 as part of CVG-7 aboard LEYTE (CV-32), in October of 1948. They operated sixteen Corsairs aboard the LEYTE, converting to the AD-3 the following year. (USN)

(Below) F4U-4 (81453) Corsair of VF-32 at Harbor Field in 1949. These types of markings with the liberal use of large quantities of White paint often denoted special roles. White has been added to the spinner, tail fin, fuselage, fuel tank, and wings. (Bern Edder via Jim Sullivan)

(Above) F4U-4 Corsair of VF-75 off the coast of Brazil during March of 1946 as part of CVBG-75 aboard MIDWAY (CVB-41). (USN/NA via Jim Sullivan)

(Above) F4U-4 of VF-113 was part of CVG-11 aboard PHILIPPINE SEA (CV-47) during late 1950 off the Coast of Korea. (USN)

(Left) F4U-4 (81624) Corsairs of Reserve VF-783 from Los Alamitos was activated during the Korean War as part of Reserve CVG-102. VF-783 was re-designated VF-122 when reserve CVG-102 was redesignated fleet CVG-12 during 1953. (USN)

(Above) F4U-4 Corsairs of VF-671 as part of CVG-8 aboard TARAWA (CV-40) in January of 1952. CVG-8 also included VF-742, VF-916, VF-921 equipped with Corsairs, and VA-859 equipped with AD-2 Skyraiders. (USN)

(Above) F4U-4 Corsairs of VF-64 (M-403) and VF-69 (M-201) whos' pilots had the misfortune of landing aboard a carrier other than BOX-ER (CV-21), to which CVG-6 was attached during 1952. (Art Schoeni)

(Below) F4U-4 (81975) Corsair of VF-74 aboard BON HOMME RICHARD (CV-31) in November of 1952. This squadron had been previously designated VBF-20, VF-10A, VF-92, and finally VF-74 on 15 February 1950. (USN)

SB2C-5 (89143) of VA9A
in 1948

SB2C-4E of VB-74,
MIDWAY (CVB-41) in 1948

SB2C-5 of VB-15A,
SAIPAN (CVL-48) in 1947

VT-17

SB2C-4E Helldiver of VT-17,
CVG-17, Brunswick in 1946

F6F-5 of VF-3,
Quonset Point in 1956

F6F-5P (80084) of
VF-75 in 1946

F6F-5N of VF(N)-51,
SHANGRI LA (CV-38) in 1945/46

F6F-5 Hellcat of VBF-20.
This is the CO's aircraft, 1946

Lower Port Wing

VF-5B

F6F-5P of VF-5B,
CORAL SEA (CVB-43) in 1948

F6F-5 (78269) of VF-111
in 1948

F6F-5 of VF-73,
Quonset Point in 1952

F6F-5N (94071) of VC-3
in 1949

VT-82

VA-20A

TBM-3E Avenger of VT-82, RANDOLPH (CV-15) in 1946

TBM-3E of VA-20A, Correy Field in 1948

TBM-3E of VA-6A in 1948

TBM-3E of VA-18A, CORAL SEA (CVB-43) in 1948

VA-15

TBM-3E (53722) Avenger of VA-15, ROOSEVELT (CVB-42) in 1949

VC-21

TBM-3E (53576) of VA-35, LAYTE (CV-32) in 1949

TBM-3S (91152) of VC-21 in 1950

TBM-3W (69476) of VS-32, PALAU (CVE-122) in 1951

TBM-3E (53775) of VS-871, Alameda in 1951

Lower Starboard

TBM-3W of VC-11 in 1950

26

F8F-1B (95130) VF-3A,
Cleveland in 1947

F8F-1 (95280) of VF-5A,
SHANGRI LA (CV-38) in 1947

F8F-1 (95001) VF-1A,
TARAWA (CV-40) in 1947

VBF-18

VF-3A

F8F-1 Bearcat of VBF-18,
LEYTE (CV-32) in 1946

F8F-2 of VF-92,
LEYTE (CV-32) in 1949

F8F-2P (121663) VC-62 in 1949

F8F-2 (121695) of VF-194,
BOXER (CV-21) in 1950

F8F-1 of VF-20A,
PHILIPPINE SEA (CV-47) in 1947

VF-20A

F8F-2 Bearcat of VF-13A, CAG-13
PRINCETON (CV-37) in 1947

F8F-1B of VF-171,
RANDOLPH (CV-15) in Oct of 1948

F8F-2 of VF-151,
ANTIETAM (CV-36) in 1949

F8F-2 (121546 of VF-72,
MIDWAY (CVB-41) in 1950

F8F-2 of VF-82 in 1952

F4U-4 (80960) of VBF-4,
NAS Chincoteague in 1946

F4U-4 of VF-75,
CAG-75 in 1946

F4U-4 (80887) of VF-22,
CORAL SEA (CVB-43) in 1948

VF-22

VF-82

F4U-4 Corsair of VF-82,
RANDOLF (CV-15) in Nov 1946

F4U-5 (121928) of VF-44,
Wilmington, NC in 1951

F4U-5 (121846), CO of CAG-1,
Cherry Point, NC in 1950

F4U-4B (62924) of VF-113,
PHILIPPINE SEA (CV-47) in 1950

F4U-5P (121977) of VC-61,
VALLEY FORGE (CV-45) in

F4U-4 Corsair of VF-193 Ghostriders,
PRINCETON (CV-37) in 1951

Typical Strike
Marks

VF-193

F4U-4 (81972) of VF-791,
BOXER (CV-21) in 1951

F4U-4 (81624) of VF-783,
BON HOMME RICHARD (CV-31) in 1951

F4U-4 (81975) of VF-74,
BON HOMME RICHARD (CV-31) in 1952

F4U-4 of VF-64,
BOXER (CV-21) in 1952

28

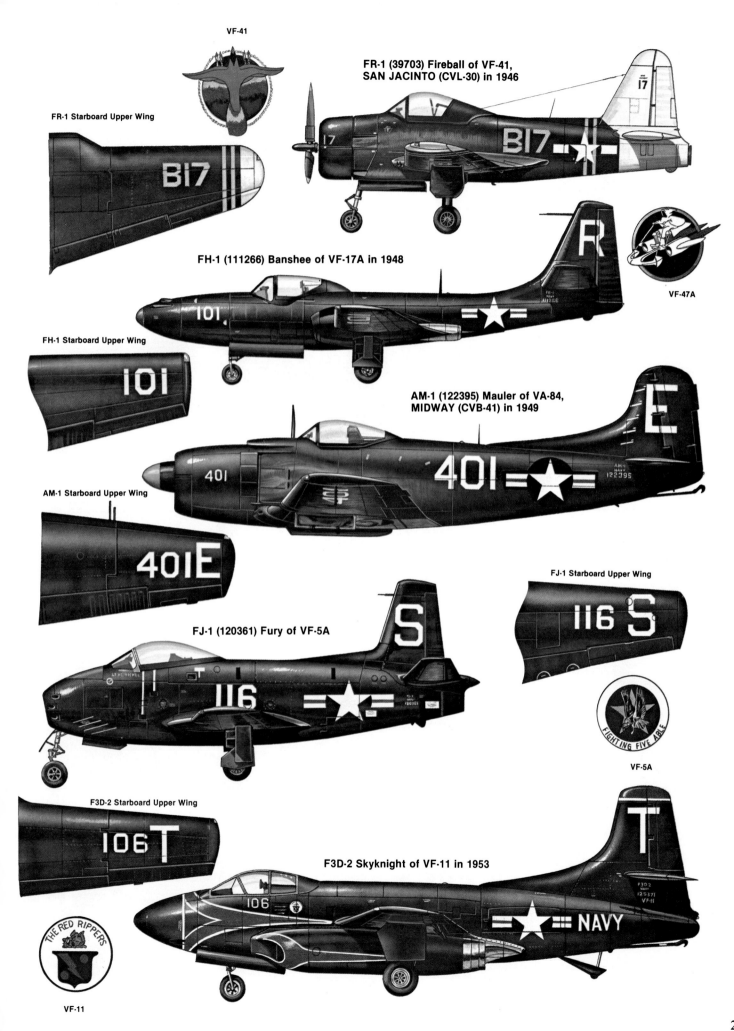

VF-41

FR-1 Starboard Upper Wing

B17

FR-1 (39703) Fireball of VF-41,
SAN JACINTO (CVL-30) in 1946

B17

FH-1 (111266) Banshee of VF-17A in 1948

VF-47A

FH-1 Starboard Upper Wing

101

AM-1 (122395) Mauler of VA-84,
MIDWAY (CVB-41) in 1949

AM-1 Starboard Upper Wing

401E

FJ-1 Starboard Upper Wing

116 S

FJ-1 (120361) Fury of VF-5A

FIGHTING FIVE ABLE

VF-5A

F3D-2 Starboard Upper Wing

106T

F3D-2 Skyknight of VF-11 in 1953

THE RED RIPPERS

VF-11

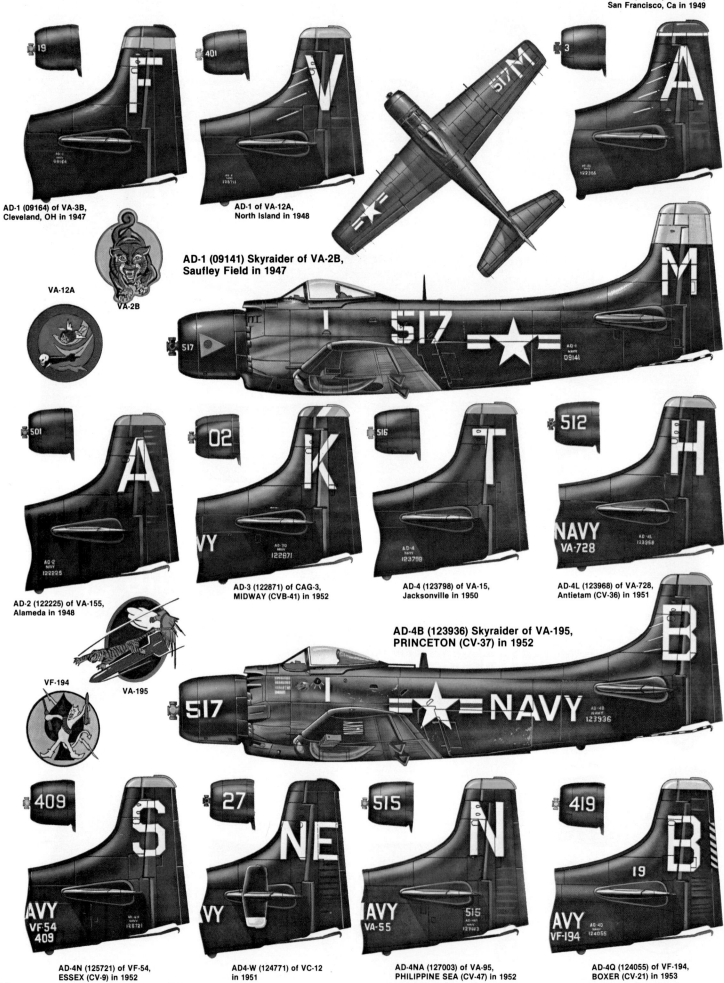

AD-2Q (122366) of VC-150,
San Francisco, Ca in 1949

AD-1 (09164) of VA-3B,
Cleveland, OH in 1947

AD-1 of VA-12A,
North Island in 1948

VA-12A

VA-2B

AD-1 (09141) Skyraider of VA-2B,
Saufley Field in 1947

AD-2 (122225) of VA-155,
Alameda in 1948

AD-3 (122871) of CAG-3,
MIDWAY (CVB-41) in 1952

AD-4 (123798) of VA-15,
Jacksonville in 1950

AD-4L (123968) of VA-728,
Antietam (CV-36) in 1951

AD-4B (123936) Skyraider of VA-195,
PRINCETON (CV-37) in 1952

VF-194

VA-195

AD-4N (125721) of VF-54,
ESSEX (CV-9) in 1952

AD4-W (124771) of VC-12
in 1951

AD-4NA (127003) of VA-95,
PHILIPPINE SEA (CV-47) in 1952

AD-4Q (124055) of VF-194,
BOXER (CV-21) in 1953

30

F2H-2 (123292) of VF-62,
CORAL SEA (CVA-43) in 1954

F2H-2 (123362) of VF-44,
INTREPID (CVA-11) in 1954

VF-44

F2H-2 (123339) Banshee of VA-76,
ATG-182 in 1955/56

F2H-2 (123340) of VF-172,
ESSEX (CV-9) in 1953

VA-76

F2H-2 (123224) of VF-34,
ANTIETAM (CVA-36) in 1953

F2H-2 (123369) of VC-4, Det 4,
MIDWAY (CVB-41) in 1952

F2H-2B (125062) of VC-3,
Korea in 1952

F2H-2B (125067) of VF-101,
MIDWAY (CVA-41) in 1954/55

VC-61

F2H-2P (128863) Banshee of VC-61,
BOXER (CV-21), Korea in 1953

VF-82

F2H-2N (123300) of VF-82,
LAKE CHAMPLAIN (CVA-39) in 1954

F2H-2P (125703) of VC-62,
MIDWAY (CVA-41) in 1954/55

F2H-2N (123307) of VC-4
in 1955

F2H-2P of VC-62,
WASP (CVA-18) in 1953

31

F9F-2 (123494) of VF-21, MIDWAY (CVB-41) in 1951

F9F-2 (121083) of VF-831, ANTIETAM (CV-36) in 1952

F9F-2 (123041) of VF-72, BON HOMME RICHARD (CV-31) in 1952

VF-831

VF-21

F9F-5 (125584) of VF-192 Golden Dragons, ORISKANY (CV-34) in 1954

F9F-2B (123668) of VF-721, BOXER (CV-21) in 1951

Upper Starboard Wing

VF-113

VF-84

STINGERS

F9F-2 (123592) of VF-91, PHILIPPINE SEA (CV-47) in 1952

F9F-2 (123490) of VF-31, LEYTE (CV-32) in 1951

F9F-2P (123567) of VC-61, Miramar in 1953

F9F-2 (123534) Panther of VF-123, PHILIPPINE SEA (CV-47) in July of 1955

F9F-5 (125962) of VF-84, LAKE CHAMPLAIN (CVA-39) in 1954

F9F-5 (125287) of VF-154, YORKTOWN (CVA-10) in 1954

F9F-5 (125572) of VF-113, BOXER (CVA-21) in 1953

F9F-5 (125550) of VF-102, TARAWA (CVA-40) in 1954

32

FJ-3 (135810) of VC-3
during Fleet Introduction
Program in 1954

FJ-3 of VF-94,
Alameda in 1955

FJ-3 (135799) Fury of VF-191 in 1956

FJ-3 (141402) of VF-121,
Miramar in 1956

VF-191

VF-62

GLADIATORS

VF-62

FJ-3 (136141) of VF-62,
ATG-202, RANDOLPH (CVA-15) in 1956

FJ-3M (141367) of VF-173,
ROOSEVELT (CVA-42) in 1956/57

FJ-3 of VF-211,
BON HOMME RICHARD (CVA-31) in 1956

FJ-3M (149230) of VF-84,
FORRESTAL (CVA-59) in 1956/57

JESTERS

VF-73

FJ-3M (141435) Fury of VF-73, RANDOLPH (CV-15) in 1956/57

V F-142

FJ-3M (146155) of VF-24,
Miramar in 1956

FJ-3 (136123) of VF-21,
ATG-181, FORRESTAL (CVA-59) in 1956

FJ-3M (141372) of VF-142,
HORNET (CVA-12) in 1956

FJ-3 (136079) of VF-143,
ATG-2 in 1956

33

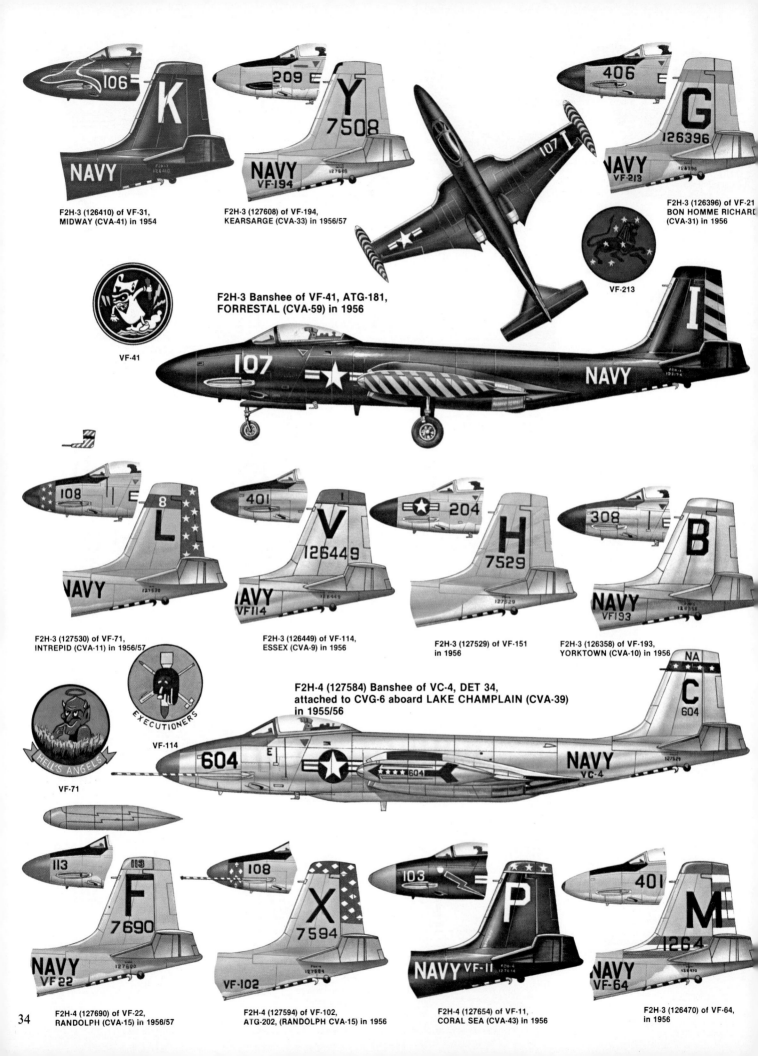

F2H-3 (126410) of VF-31,
MIDWAY (CVA-41) in 1954

F2H-3 (127608) of VF-194,
KEARSARGE (CVA-33) in 1956/57

F2H-3 (126396) of VF-21
BON HOMME RICHARD
(CVA-31) in 1956

VF-213

F2H-3 Banshee of VF-41, ATG-181,
FORRESTAL (CVA-59) in 1956

VF-41

F2H-3 (127530) of VF-71,
INTREPID (CVA-11) in 1956/57

F2H-3 (126449) of VF-114,
ESSEX (CVA-9) in 1956

F2H-3 (127529) of VF-151
in 1956

F2H-3 (126358) of VF-193,
YORKTOWN (CVA-10) in 1956

F2H-4 (127584) Banshee of VC-4, DET 34,
attached to CVG-6 aboard LAKE CHAMPLAIN (CVA-39)
in 1955/56

EXECUTIONERS

VF-114

HELL'S ANGELS

VF-71

F2H-4 (127690) of VF-22,
RANDOLPH (CVA-15) in 1956/57

F2H-4 (127594) of VF-102,
ATG-202, (RANDOLPH CVA-15) in 1956

F2H-4 (127654) of VF-11,
CORAL SEA (CVA-43) in 1956

F2H-3 (126470) of VF-64,
in 1956

34

AD-6 (134564 of VA-196,
LEXINGTON (CVA-16) in 1956/57

AD-5W of VAW-11/CVG-15,
WASP (CVA-18) in 1956

AD-6 (134594) of VA-104,
LEYETE (CVA-32) in 1955

VA-196

VA-104

AD-6 (139614) Skyraider of VA-176,
RANDOLPH (CVA-15) in 1956

AD-4N (125722) of VA-216,
BON HOMME RICHARD (CVA-31) in 1956

AD-6 of VA-105, ATG-201,
BENNINGTON (CVA-20) in 1956

AD-6 (139651) of VA-55,
in 1956

AD-5 (133929) of VA-65,
Minneapolis in 1956

AD-7 (142030) Skyraider of VA-95 in 1956

VA-95

AD-6 (137545) of VA-42,
FORRESTAL (CVA-59) in 1956

AD-6 (137596) of VA-155,
WASP (CVA-18) in 1956

AD-6 (134538) of VA-15,
SARATOGA (CVA-60) in 1956

AD-6 (137567) of VA-145,
HORNET (CVA-12) in 1956/57

35

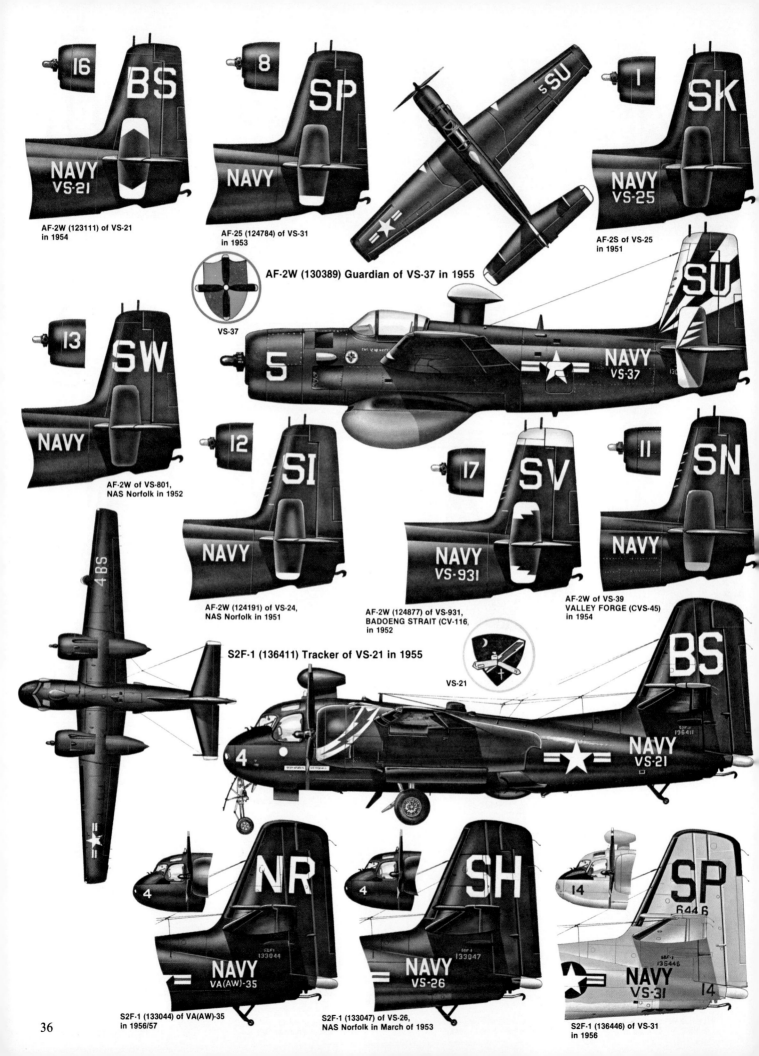

AF-2W (123111) of VS-21
in 1954

AF-25 (124784) of VS-31
in 1953

AF-2S of VS-25
in 1951

AF-2W (130389) Guardian of VS-37 in 1955

VS-37

AF-2W of VS-801,
NAS Norfolk in 1952

AF-2W (124191) of VS-24,
NAS Norfolk in 1951

AF-2W (124877) of VS-931,
BADOENG STRAIT (CV-116,
in 1952

AF-2W of VS-39
VALLEY FORGE (CVS-45)
in 1954

S2F-1 (136411) Tracker of VS-21 in 1955

VS-21

S2F-1 (133044) of VA(AW)-35
in 1956/57

S2F-1 (133047) of VS-26,
NAS Norfolk in March of 1953

S2F-1 (136446) of VS-31
in 1956

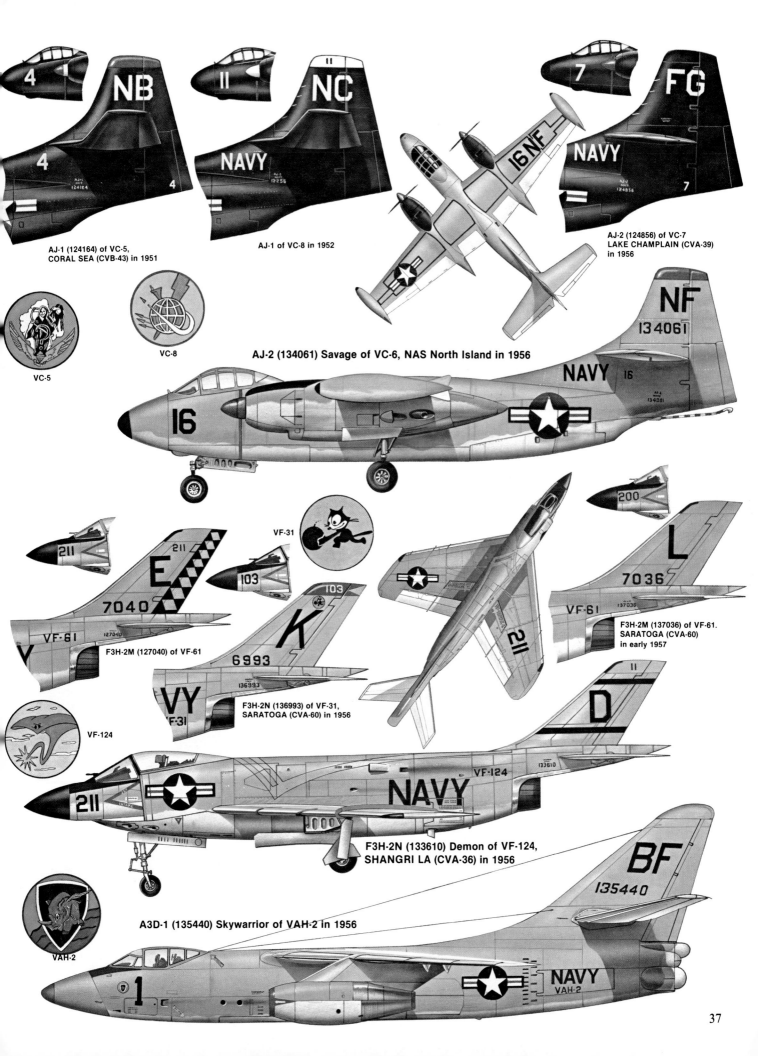

AJ-1 (124164) of VC-5,
CORAL SEA (CVB-43) in 1951

AJ-1 of VC-8 in 1952

AJ-2 (124856) of VC-7
LAKE CHAMPLAIN (CVA-39)
in 1956

VC-5

VC-8

AJ-2 (134061) Savage of VC-6, NAS North Island in 1956

VF-31

F3H-2M (127040) of VF-61

F3H-2N (136993) of VF-31,
SARATOGA (CVA-60) in 1956

F3H-2M (137036) of VF-61.
SARATOGA (CVA-60)
in early 1957

VF-124

F3H-2N (133610) Demon of VF-124,
SHANGRI LA (CVA-36) in 1956

A3D-1 (135440) Skywarrior of VAH-2 in 1956

VAH-2

37

F4D-1 (134777) of VC-3,
Moffett Field in 1956

F4D-1 (134808) of VF-141,
ESSEX (CV-9) in 1956

F4D-1 of VF-101,
ATG-201 in 1956

BE-DEVILERS

VF-74

F4D-1 (134816) Skyray of VF-74, late 1956

F9F-6 (128193) of VF-123
in 1954

F9F-6 (127339) of VF-142,
HANCOCK (CV-19) in 1954

F9F-6 (130951) of VF-61

VF-24

VF-91

F9F-6 (131054) Cougar of VF-24 aboard YORKTOWN (CV-10)
in October of 1953

F9F-6 (130985) of VF-33,
MIDWAY (CVB-41) in 1954

F9F-6 (127340) of VF-91,
HORNET (CV-12) in 1954

F9F-6 (127383) of VF-191,
ORISKANY (CV-34) in 1954

F9F-7 (130797) of VF-21,
NAS Oceana in 1953

F9F-8 (131178) of VF-74,
LAKE CHAMPLAIN (CVA-39) in 1955/56

F9F-8 (141148) of VF-13,
Cecil Field in 1954

F9F-8 (131125) of VF-121,
Alameda in 1956

F9F-8 (141073) Cougar of VF-112 in 1956

VF-112

VF-13

F9F-8 (144308) of VA-144
HORNET (CVA-12) in 1956/57

F9F-8 (144354) of VF-81,
ATG-182 in 1956

F9F-8 (141666) of VA-44,
RANDOLPH (CVA-15) in 1956

F9F-8 (141657) of VA-146,
HORNET (CVA-12) in 1956/57

F9F-8 (141128) Cougar of VF-123 in 1956

BITTER BIRDS

VF-144

VF-123

"THE BLUE RACERS"

F9F-8 of VF-13,
ATG-201 in 1956

F9F-8 (141124) of VF-61,
INTREPID (CVA-11) in 1956

F9F-8 (141123) of VA-76,
ATG-182 in 1956

F9F-8P (144379) of VC-62,
Jacksonville in 1956

39

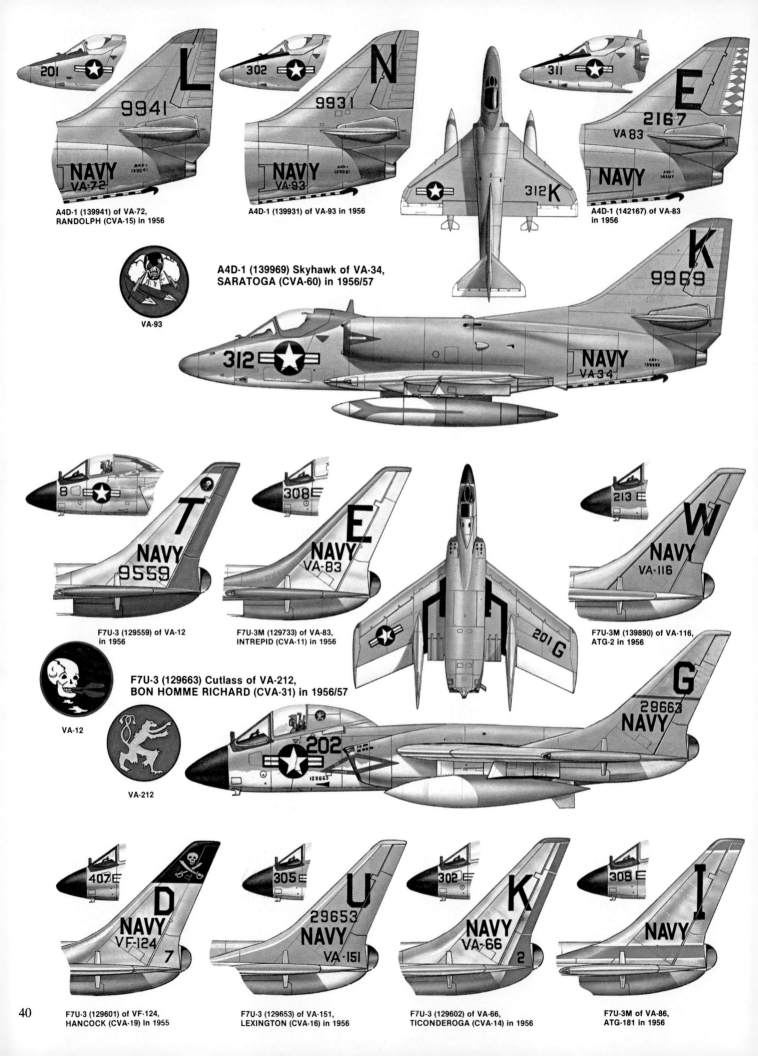

A4D-1 (139941) of VA-72,
RANDOLPH (CVA-15) in 1956

A4D-1 (139931) of VA-93 in 1956

A4D-1 (142167) of VA-83
in 1956

VA-93

A4D-1 (139969) Skyhawk of VA-34,
SARATOGA (CVA-60) in 1956/57

F7U-3 (129559) of VA-12
in 1956

F7U-3M (129733) of VA-83,
INTREPID (CVA-11) in 1956

F7U-3M (139890) of VA-116,
ATG-2 in 1956

VA-12

F7U-3 (129663) Cutlass of VA-212,
BON HOMME RICHARD (CVA-31) in 1956/57

VA-212

F7U-3 (129601) of VF-124,
HANCOCK (CVA-19) In 1955

F7U-3 (129653) of VA-151,
LEXINGTON (CVA-16) in 1956

F7U-3 (129602) of VA-66,
TICONDEROGA (CVA-14) in 1956

F7U-3M of VA-86,
ATG-181 in 1956

F8F BEARCAT - The F8F Bearcat, while considered obsolete with the arrival of jet aircraft, remained in the fighter-bomber role since these early jets lacked sufficient bomb carrying capability. F8F Bearcats equipped a total of twenty-four squadrons as the F8F-1, -1B and -2, reached a peak in 1949 before being phased out in 1952.

(Below) F8F-1B Bearcat of VF-17 flying over Quonset Point in late 1946 as part of CVGB-17 which was operating from Coral Sea (CVB-43). Identification markings C103 and 103 are in Yellow. (Ernie McDowell)

(Above) F8F-1 Bearcat of VF-18 in August of 1946. The Yellow Y on the tail fin is not a carrier code, but a flight section code. This type of tail code usage seems to have been adopted by only a few CVGs. (Pete Bowers Collection)

F8F-1 (94788) Bearcat of VF-19, the first squadron to operate the Bearcat, was assigned to the ANTIETAM (CV-36). Both carrier and aircraft ID codes were in Yellow, April of 1946. (Bill Larkins)

F8F-1 (95001) Bearcat of VF-1A (became VF-11 in 1948) Red Rippers from CVAG-13 aboard TARAWA (CV-40) during June of 1947. The CAG's aircraft has the centerline fuel tank carrying the squadron colors on its tip. (Bill Larkins)

These F8F-2 Bearcats of VF-82 during August of 1952 aboard MID-WAY (CVB-41) illustrates the addition of high visibility service markings on the fuselage introduced in May of 1950, as well as a larger bureau number and aircraft designator under the horizontal tail plane. (D.Walsh via Bill Larkins)

(Above) F8F-2 Bearcats of VF-112 from MIDWAY (CVB-41) carrying special White war game exercise markings. (USN)

(Above) F8F-1 Bearcats of VF-10A during 1947 carrying one of the few double letter carrier air group codes then in use. The PS is a carry over from PHILIPPINE SEA (CV-47). (Fred Roos Collection)

(Above) F-8F-1 (95261) of VF-5A aboard BOXER (CV-21) in March of 1948. The squadron was also working with the FJ-1 Fury and phased out the Bearcat after this cruise. (Pete Bowers Collection)

(Below) F8F-1 Bearcat of VF-15A landing aboard TARAWA (CV-40) in July of 1948. The squadron and CVAG-15 were de-commissioned in December of 1949. When CVAG-15 was re-commissioned in April of 1951 the air group was assigned the tail code H. (Clay Jansson)

FR FIREBALL - The Ryan FR-1 Fireball, combining both a jet and prop engine, was only operational with World War II squadron VF-66 which was redesignated VF-41 in October of 1945, and finally VF-1E before being phased out in 1947. The Fireball was equipped with four machine guns, two wing racks for 1000 pound bombs, and two wing racks for rockets.

(Below) FR-1 Fireball of VF-66 during its first public showing in October of 1945. (Bill Wagner)

FH PHANTOM and FJ FURY - The first jet airplane arrived in July of 1947 when the McDonnell FH-1 Phantom entered the Fleet with VA-17A (became VF-171 in 1948). Next in the Navy's transition to jet powered aircraft was the North American FJ-1 Fury, entering service with VF-5A (became VF-51 in 1948) during November of 1947. Within two years these same squadrons were re-equipped with what would become the basic carrier fighters of the Korean War. First was the McDonnell F2H Banshee followed by the Grumman F9F Panther, both in 1949.

(Above) FH-1 Phantom of VF-17A (became VF-171 in 1948) recovering aboard FRANKLIN D ROOSEVELT (CVB-42) in May of 1947. VF-17A was the only squadron to operate the Navy's first pure jet. (MDAC via Fred Roos)

AM MAULER - The Martin AM-1 Mauler entered Fleet service with VA-17A (became VA-174 in 1948) during March of 1948, three months after the AD Skyraider. It served with five squadrons before being phased out in 1950 in favor of the Skyraider.

(Above) FJ-1 (120361) Fury of VF-5A being brought up on the side elevator of BOXER (CV-21) in preparation for a launch during March of 1948. (USN via Clay Jansson)

(Below) AM-1 (22299) Mauler of VA-174 at Quonset Point in 1948. Four VA and one VC squadrons were equipped with the Mauler before the Navy replaced it with the AD Skyraider. (Jim Sullivan Collection)

AD SKYRAIDER - The Douglas AD-1 Skyraider was the first new aircraft type to enter fleet service after the end of World War II, arriving during December of 1946 with VA-19A (became VA-193 in 1948) of the Pacific Fleet. The Atlantic Fleet, VA-3B and VA-4B (became VA-44 and VA-45 respectively in 1948), received their first Skyraiders in April of the following year. By 1947 there were eight squadrons operating the Skyraider. The AD-2 entered the Fleet in 1949, followed in 1950 by the AD-3 and the AD-4, which would become the version most widely used during the Korean War. Additional attack versions of the Skyraider were added, the AD-4B with nuclear capability, the winterized AD-4L for operating in cold weather, and the AD-4NA day attack version. During the Korean War twenty attack squadrons (VAs) operated the AD with the 7th Fleet. The AD-6, an improved version of the AD-4B with a low altitude bombing system, first entered Fleet service with VA-35 in late 1953. When shore based, each squadron was assigned an AD-5 for training and utility activities.

(Above) An AD-2Q (122366) Skyraider of VC-150, the aircraft number denotes aircraft from the CAG-15 commander's aircraft pool. This scheme was introduced in August of 1948. The propeller hub and top of the vertical fin are Red bordered in White. Photo taken in October of 1949. (Bill Larkins)

(Below) XBT2D-1 (09100), one of the Skyraider prototypes, assigned to VA-1L carrying the tail codes orginally belonging to SAIPAN (CVL-48), and later to CVLG-1 when this photograph was taken in 1948. Other aircraft in use by VF-1L at this time included six TBM-3E Avengers and a SNJ-4. (Tom Cuddy II)

AD-1 Skyraiders of VA-44 from CVG-4 aboard FRANKLIN D ROOSEVELT (CVB-42) in 1949. (MDAC via Harry Gann)

AD-3 (122799) Skyraider of VA-95 at Oakland in October of 1953, the squadron had just finished a cruise aboard PHILIPPINE SEA (CVA-47) in July. By this time all CVGs had a fifth squadron normally equipped with ADs, carrying 500 series nose numbers, and Green trim. (Bill Larkins)

AD-1 (09223) Skyraider of VA-65 at the National Air Races in Cleveland during the summer of 1949. VA-65 insignia is carried below the cockpit, but VF-61 has zapped the cowling of the CAG's aircraft with their Jolly Roger insignia. (Bill Larkins)

AD-2 (122248) Skyraider of Reserve VA-923 in late 1950 as part of the newly commissioned reserve CVG-102. They were redesignated Fleetsquadron VA-125 in 1953. All reserve VA squadrons called up were equipped with the Skyraider. (John Woods via Fred Roos)

AD-6 (137618) Skyraider of VA-65 at Oakland in September of 1955 carries its colorful Green and White trim on the nose cowl, and vertical fin and rudder. These type of trim markings were used by the squadrons of CVG-2 during their ESSEX (CVA-9) cruise of 1954/55. (Bill Larkins via Roger Besecker)

(Below) AD-6 (137613) of VA-75 at New York City after completing a cruise aboard HORNET (CVA-12) in late 1956. (Bill Larkins Collection)

(Above) AD-6 (134594) of VA-104 with International Orange trim on the vertical fin tip, horizontal stablizer tip, and wing tip in 1956. (John Fahey via Fred Roos)

(Below) AD-6 (135366) Skyraider of VF-54 in August of 1954. While VF-54 was designated the fourth fighter squadron in the CVG, it was equipped with Skyraider bombers. This is a carry over from the Korean War when there was a shortage of ADs and some fighter squadrons operated fighter-bombers and received the VF designation for what was essentially an attack slot. (Bill Larkins)

45

F2H BANSHEE - The F2H-1 Banshee first entered service in March of 1949 with VF-171, and arrived in Korea in August with VF-172. The F2H-2 had provisions for wing tip tanks, a stretched fuselage and wing racks for bombs. Banshee fighter versions included the -2B nuclear fighter, -2N night fighter, -3 all-weather fighter, and the -4 the final fighter version. At the close of 1956 there were sixteen squadrons of Banshees. In addition Banshees were used aboard ASW carriers in four plane DETs to provide combat air protection (CAP) for the defenseless VS and HS squadrons.

(Below) F2H-2 (125052) Banshee of VF-12 tied down at Cecil Field in June of 1954. All markings are in White. (Dave Ostrowski via Fred Roos)

(Above) F2H-1 (123000) of VF-171, the first Banshee squadron at NAS Columbus during 1949. (John Durand)

(Left) F2H-2 (123333) Banshee of VF-31 landing aboard the LEYTE (CV-32) in late 1952 during a Mediterranean cruise. (Peter Bowers Collection)

(Below) F2H-2 Banshees of VF-22 flying off the coast of Japan from LAKE CHAMPLAIN (CVA-39) during July of 1953 as part of CVG-4. (MDAC via Fred Roos)

F2H-2 Banshee of VF-172 Blue Bolt taxiing aboard ESSEX (CVA-9) off the coast of Korea in September of 1951. The national insignia being applied to the forward nose rather than the aircraft number was practiced on the Banshee for only a short period. (MDAC via Fred Roos)

This F2H-3 (126437) Banshee of VF-114, The Executioners, is painted overall in aluminum paint with orange trim, during 1953. The overall application of aluminum paint was done on an experimental basis during the mid-1950s (Duane Kasulka Collection)

F2H-3 (126470) Banshee of VF-64 at Santa Rosa during the summer of 1956 before deploying aboard SHANGRI–LA (CV-38) in November. Trim colors are Orange and White. (Pete Bowers via Jim Sullivan)

(Above) A pair of F2H-3 Banshees of VF-152 in a natural metal finish fly above the YORKTOWN (CVA-10) during 1954. Natural metal aircraft were part of an experiment in aircraft color schemes conducted during 1954, and culminated in the Light Gray over White scheme introduced during 1955. (USN/NA)

(Below) F2H-4 (127603) Banshees of VF-82 Ironmen in 1955. Markings carried on the forward nose are the 200 series numbers of the second squadron in CVG-8. (John Durand)

(Left) F2H-4 (137521) of VF-193 flying from YORKTOWN (CVA-10) in early 1957. This was the third set of markings applied to VF-193's Banshees in as many years. (USN/NA)

(Below) F2H-3 (127520) Banshee of VF-71 at Moffett Field in May of 1956 painted in the new Light Gray over White scheme that opened the way for the addition of very colorful trim colors. On 108 the nose and rudder are painted Red with White stars. (Bill Larkins via Fred Roos)

F9F PANTHER - The Panther followed the Banshee into service in May of 1949 when the F9F-3 equipped VF-51. The next version, the -2 was similar to the -3 except for a different engine, which was later retrofitted to the -3, after which the -3s were redesignated -2s. The *Sundowners* of VF-111 introduced the -2 to fleet service in December. The next variation was the F9F-2B *fighter-bomber* with the addition of six underwing pylons for bombs and rockets were added. This first Navy jet fighter-bomber arrived in April of 1951 with VF-191. All F9F-2Bs were later redesignated -2s when all -2s were brought up to 2B standards by retrofitting them with the six underwing pylons. The

F9F-4 had a larger fuselage and enlarged tail section, while the -5 received a more powerful engine in the -4 airframe. An interesting sidelight was the re-introduction of the F6F-5 Hellcat into the Fleet when F9F-5 Panther engines developed problems and was delayed in its delivery to the Fleet. Several squadrons flew the Hellcat as an interim aircraft during 1953, VF-73 being the last squadron to fly the F6F when they finally phased the Hellcat out of service in August of 1953. The final straight winged Panther, the -5 was phased out in late 1955; VA-36, VA-72, and VF-92 were the last to operate the Panther.

F9F-3 (123073) Panther of VF-52 during 1951. The trim color is White. (Grumman Aerospace Corp)

F9F-2 Panthers of VF-71 heading back to their carrier after a strike against targets in North Korea during 1952. (USN/NA)

F9F-2B (123713) of VF-721 over Korea in September of 1951 as part of reserve CVG-101. VF-721 was re-designated VF-141 when its parent, reserve CVG-101, became fleet CVG-14 in 1953. (Grumman Aerospace Corp)

(Above) F9F-5 (125099) Panther of VF-837 at Buchanan Field in May of 1951. VF-837 was activated from the reserves in February of 1951 and redesignated to VF-154 in 1953. (Bill Larkins)

(Below) F9F-5 Panthers of VF-154 carrying Yellow lightning bolts and trim colors during the WestPac cruise aboard YORKTOWN (CVA-10) in late 1954. (USN/NA via Jim Sullivan)

(Above) F9F-5 (127206) of VF-24 aboard BOXER (CV-21) off the coast of Korea in May of 1952. Trim color is Yellow. CVG-2 tail code M is also carried on the lower starboard wing. (Arthur Schoeni)

(Above) F9F-5s of VF-192 Golden Dragons aboard the ORISKANY (CVA-34) during 1954. The dragon painted on the nose of squadron aircraft was in Gold. The special war game markings were applied in a washable White paint. (USN/NA)

(Below) F9F-5 (126034) Panther of VF-781 recovering aboard ORISKANY (CVA-34) in November of 1952. VF-781 was re-designated to VF-121 in 1953. (USN/NA via Jim Sullivan)

F3D SKYKNIGHT - The all-weather Douglas F3D-2 Skyknight had entered the Fleet with composite squadron VC-3 in February of 1951, but it was 1953 before the Skyknight was assigned to *Fleet* fighter squadrons, first with VF-11 *Red Rippers* and followed by VF-14 *Top Hatters*. Neither squadron actually deployed for a cruise with the Skyknight since the Navy considered it too large for carrier duty.

F3D-2 (127072) Skyknight of VF-14 Tophatters preparing to land aboard INTREPID (CVA-11) in September of 1954; VF-14 was attached to Air Task Group 201. The only other fighter squadron to operate the Skyknight was VF-11 Red Rippers. (USN)

FJ-3 FURY - The North American FJ-2 Fury, a Navy copy of the Air Force's F-86 Sabre, was considered less suitable for carrier operations than the swept wing F9F-6 Cougar. In January of 1954 the FJ-2 Furys were turned over to Marine VMF squadrons. The FJ-3 Fury was a new design from North America with improved carrier suitability over the earlier -2 Fury and in September of 1954 VF-173 became the first operational squadron to equip with the new fighter. The FJ-3M was a missile equipped version of the Fury. By 1957 there were thirteen squadrons of the -3 and -3M Furys in Fleet service.

(Right) FJ-3 Fury of VF-33 Argonauts carrying White markings and trim at Miami in May of 1955. They deployed aboard LAKE CHAMPLAIN (CVA-39) in September for a Mediterranean cruise. (Clay Jansson)

(Below) FJ-3s of VF-121 flying near Miramar marked with a Yellow tail section and lightning bolt, outlined in Black. The D of CVG-12 is in White. (USN/NA)

(Below) FJ-3 Fury of VF-62 in the new Light Gray over White scheme with Red trim at Cecil Field in March of 1956. Attached to ATG-202, they had just returned from a Caribbean shakedown cruise aboard RANDOLPH (CVA-15). (Tailhook)

FJ-3 (139259) of VF-142 at Mines Field in June of 1956. Trim is Black rather than the Orange-Yellow usually carried by the second squadron of an air group. The Black trim color was used when VF-142 was originally designated VA-96, and was retained when the squadron was re-designated VF-142 and assigned as the second squadron in CVG-14. (Bill Larkins Collection)

FJ-3 (141435) of VF-73 from RANDOLPH (CVA-15) in March of 1957. The fuselage flash is Light Blue with a Black outline and the tail checkers are Light Blue and White. (USN/NA)

(Below) FJ-3 (139224) Fury of VF-84, and a F9F-8B (141042) Cougar of VA-76 attached to ATG-182 aboard FORRESTAL (CVA-59) in late 1956. (USN/NA)

An overall Dark Blue FJ-3 (136008) of VF-51 with a Red flash running the length of the fuselage and White bands and markings seen just before being deployed aboard KEARSARGE (CVA-33) in late 1955. (Bill Larkins)

FJ-3 (139229) of VF-143 attached to ATG-2 during the fall of 1956. ATG-2's W code is carried in Black on the tail. (Bill Larkins Collection)

F9F COUGAR - The Grumman F9F-6 Cougar was an attempt to improve the Panther's performance by sweeping the wings and horizontal stabilizers, and adding a new more powerful engine. The *Swordsmen* of VF-32 were the first to equip, receiving the F9F-6 Cougar during November of 1952. The -7 used the same airframe as the -6 but with a different engine and was instrumented to operate only as a day fighter. The -8 had a larger wing with six under wing pylons, an enlarged tail, and provisions for in-flight refueling, with VF-13 being the first Fleet squadron to receive them in 1954. The -6 was phased out by VA-156 in late 1956. The final version was a modification performed by the Navy on the basic -8 by adding a low-altitude bombing system under the designation -8B.

(Right) F9F-6 Cougars of VF-153 off of YORKTOWN (CVA-10) in December of 1954 flying over Mount Fuji, Japan. Trim colors are White. (USN/NA)

(Above) F9F-8 (131197) Cougar of VF-122 from SHANGRI-LA (CVA-38) in 1956. (Bill Larkins Collection)

(Below) F9F-6 (131047) of VF-21 in Red and White trim as part of CVG-2. (Grumman Aeronautics via H J Schonenberg)

(Above) F9F-7 (130797) Cougar of VF-21 from NAS Oceana in October of 1953. Only a few carrier squadrons operated the -7 Cougar. (USN/NA via Jim Sullivan)

(Below) F9F-8 (141035) of VF-53 at Yokota, Japan in May of 1956. Fin cap trim is Light Blue with White trim on wing tips, trailing edge of wings, rudder, and aft fuselage. (USAF via O R Zeisloft)

(Above) F9F-8 (141212) Cougar of VA-46 Clansmen carrying ATG-202 tail code during 1956. The Clansmen's original skipper was Scottish and the squadron adopted his clan colors on the fin of their aircraft. (Lional Paul Collection)

(Below) F9F-8B of VF-81 Crusaders attached to ATG-182 prior to cruise aboard LAKE CHAMPLAIN (CVA-39) to the Mediterranean in early 1957. The Crusaders were commissioned in July of 1955 as an all-weather intercepter squadron, then in January of 1956 were assigned the new mission of special weapons delivery. In December they were designated as a fighter squadron. (USN)

CAG-4 F9F-8 Cougar being brought up on one of Saratoga's elevators in August of 1956. Trim colors on the tail from left to right are Yellow, Red, Medium Blue, and Orange. (USN/NA via Stan Piet Jr.)

F7U CUTLASS - The most radical fighter to enter service during this time frame was the twin engined Chance Vought F7U-3 Cutlass. The first squadron to equip with the Cutlass was VF-81 in April of 1954. The Cutlass was the Navy's first aircraft to be equipped with an afterburner, and the -3 which was followed by the -3M equipped with Sparrow I missiles and was first deployed overseas with VA-83 in March of 1956. Initially some Cutlass equipped VF squadrons were redesignated VA squadrons in anticipation of the fighter-bomber version that was to be designated A2U-1. However this attack version of the Cutlass was cancelled in late 1954 and the -3M version was introduced to these squadrons instead.

F7U-3 (129676) of VA-212, the second squadron in the newly commissioned CVG-21. This is the squadron CO's aircraft and has just landed aboard BON HOMME RICHARD (CVA-31) during carrier quals in July of 1956. (USN/NA)

(Below) F7U-3M of VF-83 in natural metal as were most Cutlass aircraft. VF-83 was the first squadron equipped with the F7U-3M Cutlass carrying Sparrow Missiles. (Bob Esposito)

In natural metal, this F7U-3 Cutlass of VF-124, with afterburners lit, is ready to launch from HANCOCK (CVA-19) during 1956. The F7U was the Navy's first aircraft with afterburners. (USN via Larry Kasulka)

(Below) F7U-3 (129623) Cutlass of VA-34 carrying Dark Blue trim colors. A hard landing blew a tire and the Cutlass ran off the runway at Cecil Field in July of 1956. (Jack Anderson)

F3H DEMON - The McDonnell all-weather F3H-2N Demon was introduced into the Fleet by the *Tophatters* of VF-14 in March of 1956. They were quickly joined by four more Demon squadrons before the end of the year. The F3H Demon was equipped with four 20MM cannons and pylons for four Sidewinder air-to-air missiles.

F3H-2 (137040) Demon of VF-61 carrying 200 series nose numbers, with the squadron Yellow and Black diamond trim being carried on the tail. (MDAC via Fred Harl)

F3H-2 (133588) Demon of VF-14 awaiting parking on the bow. The Top Hatters were the first carrier fighter squadron to equip with the Demon. Trim color is Red. (MDAC)

F4D SKYRAY - The first Squadron to receive the all-weather Douglas F4D-1 Skyray were the *Be-Devilers* of VF-74 in April of 1956. By the end of the year three additional Skyray squadrons were added to the Fleet. The Skyray was initially equipped with air-to-air ballistic rockets, which were removed in favor of the Sidewinder missile.

F4D-1 of VF-101, which was part of CVG-10, but was assigned to ATG-201 while transitioning to the Skyray. (MDAC via Harry Gann)

A4D SKYHAWK - The Douglas A4D-1 Skyhawk was introduced to the Fleet by VA-72 in October of 1956. The Skyhawk was the Navy's first tactical jet attack aircraft and was capable of nuclear weapons delivery. To achieve this the A4D-1 carried a bomb-shaped electronic pod to provide navigation and bombing aids. By the end of the year VA-93 had also re-equipped with the Skyhawk, with VA-34 and VA-83 starting their transition into the new fighter.

A4D-1 (139940) Skyhawk from the Blue Hawks of VA-72 during Skyhawk carrier quals aboard RANDOLPH (CVA-15) in 1956. The Blue Hawks was the first attack squadron to equip with the A4D. (MDAC via Harry Gann)

VA-34 was transitioning to the Skyhawk when CVG tail codes were changed to a double letter series. Many squadrons, however, continued to operate the single letter tail codes until mid-1957 when the change to double letters became mandatory. (MDAC via Harry Gann)

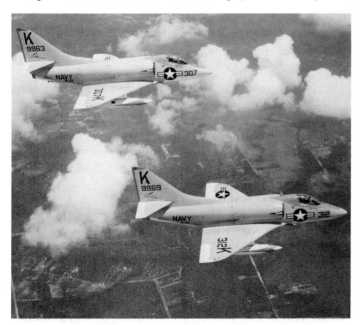

Douglas F4D-1 (134756) Skyray of VF-74, the first Skyray squadron to enter the Fleet. This photograph was take just after the squadron received their F4Ds in April of 1956, they were soon to become one of the most colorful squadrons in the fleet. (John Durand)

A4D-1 (142167) of VA-83, the fourth attack squadron to receive the Skyhawk in early 1957. Markings were CVG-8 diamonds in Blue on a field of White. (Roger Besecker Collection)

FIGHTER AND ATTACK
WITH PARENT CVG (Dec 1956)

CVG-1 "T"	CVG-2 "M"	CVG-3 "K"	CVG-4 "F"
VF-11 F2H-4	VF-23 F4D-1	VF-31 F3H-2N	VF-22 F2H-4
VA-12 F7U-3	VA-24 FJ-3	VF-32 F9F-8B	VF-43 F9F-8
VF-13 F9F-8B	VA-63 F9F-8	VF-33 FJ-3/3M	VA-44 F9F-8
VF-14 F3H-2N	VF-64 F2H-3	VA-34 F7U-3	VF-62 FJ-3/3M
VF-15 AD-6	VA-65 AD-6	VA-35 AD-6	VA-42 AD-6
VA-16 AD-6	VA-26 F9F-8/8B	VA-36 F9F-8B	VA-46 F9F-8B
CVG-5 "S"	**CVG-6 "C"**	**CVG-7 "L"**	**CVG-8 "E"**
VF-51 FJ-3M	VF-21 FJ-3M	VF-71 F2H-3	VF-81 F9F-8B
VF-52 F2H-3	VF-41 F2H-3	VA-72 A4D-1	VF-82 F2H-4
VF-53 FJ-3	VF-61 F3H-2M	VF-73 FJ-3/3M	VA-83 F7U-3M
VA-54 AD-6	VA-25 AD-6	VF-74 F4D-1	VF-84 FJ-3M
VA-55 AD-6/7	VA-42 AD-6	VA-75 AD-6	VA-85 AD-6
VA-56 F9F-8/8B	VA-66 F9F-8B	VA-76 F9F-8B	VA-86 F7U-3M
CVG-9 "N"	**CVG-10 "P"**	**CVG-11 "V"**	**CVG-12 "D"**
VF-91 FJ-3	VF-101 F4D-1	VF-111 F9F-8/8B	VF-121 FJ-3M
VF-92 F2H-3	VF-102 F2H-4	VF-112 F9F-8B	VF-122 F3H-2N
VA-93 A4D-1	VF-103 F9F-8	VA-113 F9F-8B	VF-123 F9F-8
VF-94 F9F-8B	VA-104 AD-6	VF-114 F2H-3	VF-124 F3H-2N
VA-95 AD-6/7	VA-105 AD-6	VA-115 AD-6	VA-125 AD-6
VA-96 AD-6	VA-106 F9F-8B	VA-116 F7U-3M	VA-126 F7U-3
CVG-14 "A"	**CVG-15 "H"**	**CVG-17 "R"**	**CVG-19 "B"**
VF-141 F4D-1	VA-151 F9F-8B	VF-171 F2H-3/4	VF-191 FJ-3
VF-142 FJ-3/3M	VF-152 F2H-3	VA-172 F2H-2	VA-192 F9F-8B
VF-143 FJ-3M	VA-153 F9F-8B	VF-173 FJ-3M	VF-193 F2H-3
VF-144 F9F-8	VF-154 FJ-3	VF-174 F9F-8B	VF-194 F2H-3
VA-145 AD-6	VA-155 AD-6/7	VA-175 AD-6	VA-195 AD-6
VA-146 F9F-8	VA-156 F9F-6/8B	VA-176 AD-6	VA-196 AD-6

CVG-21 "G"		
VF-211 FJ-3M		
VA-212 F7U-3	**Air Task Groups**	
VF-213 F2H-3		
VA-214 F9F-8T	ATG-1 "U"	ATG-2 "W"
VA-215 AD-6	ATG-3 "Y"	ATG-4 "Z"
VA-216 AD-7	ATG-181 "I"	ATG-182 "O"
	ATG-201 "J"	ATG-202 "X"

COMPOSITE HEAVY ATTACK

At the end of World War II the Navy found itself without a carrier based nuclear strike capability and a fleet being rapidly reduced in size. To correct this, in June of 1946 the Navy awarded a contract to North American Aviation for the AJ Savage, a twin engine carrier aircraft capable of carrying 10,000 pounds of conventional ordnance or the nuclear *Fat Boy* atomic bomb that was dropped on Nagasaki, Japan. Since the AJ-1 Savage would not be available until 1949, the Navy sought an interim aircraft to achieve a carrier based nuclear strike capability. The only aircraft with a chance of getting off a carrier deck with a 10,000 pound bomb load was the Lockheed P2V Neptune. On 28 April 1948 two specially modified P2V-2s assisted by JATO lifted off the CORAL SEA's deck. This interim nuclear carrier bomber was especially modified for carrier duty and was ordered by the Navy under the designation P2V-3C. In September VC-5 was commissioned as the first squadron equipped with the land based P2V-2, -3, and the carrier version P2V-3C. Initially the P2V-3Cs were flown to an overseas base, then hoisted aboard a carrier and flown off when at sea. One P2V-3C was fitted with arresting gear for evaluation of carrier landings which were successful. However the project was dropped since the first AJ-1 Savage arrived in

March of 1950 for fleet duty with VC-5, with the first Savage deployment taking place in February of the following year.

Additional squadrons were commissioned and equipped with P2V Neptunes and AJ Savages. With increased numbers of AJ-1s available, three plane DETs were readied for deployment and became common aboard MIDWAY and revised ESSEX class carriers. Experiments were made to test the advisability of operating these carriers with only a heavy attack unit aboard along with sufficient fighters to provide local protection. The operation proved feasible, but met difficulties in hanger and deck operations because of the aircraft's size. The improved AJ- Savage was introduced but the majority of these were converted for long range reconnaissance under the designation AJ-2P and assigned to heavy photographic squadrons (VJs). The remaining AJ Savages were equipped with a tanker package which permitted the Savage to double as an aerial tanker. Though the AJs were never used as a conventional bomber in Korea, VC-5 maintained a DET armed with nuclear weapons as a deterrent during the Korean war.

In July of 1955 those squadrons originally designated as composite heavy attack squadrons (VCs) were redesignated to VAH. The pending arrival of the new Douglas A3D-1 Skywarrior led to the Navy commissioning five heavy attack squadrons under the designation VAH, beginning with VAH-1 in November. The Navy received their first A3Ds in March of the following year.

(Above) P2V-3C (122942) Neptune of VC-6 during 1951. The JATO rack on the fuselage partially obscures the national insignia. (Roger Besecker Collection)

(Left) P2V-2 Neptune of VC-5 landing at Moffett Field in September of 1948. Aircraft is overall Gloss Dark Blue with all markings in White (Bill Larkins Collection)

(Below Left) This AJ-1 Savage is part of a DET from VC-5 stationed at the Korean air base K-3 in July of 1953. This DET was nuclear armed as a deterrent to the invading communist forces. (Clay Jansson)

(Below) AJ-1 (124175) Savage of VC-5 aboard MIDWAY (CVB-41) in November of 1951 carrying war exercise markings identifying it as part of the aggressor force. (USN/NA)

(Above) A3D-1 (135421) Skywarrior of VAH-1 from Jacksonville in September of 1956. The Skywarrior was one of three new Douglas Aircraft introduced to the Fleet during 1956. (USN/NA)

(Above) AJ-2 (122597) Savage of VAH-5 refueling an F9F-8 (141101) Cougar of VF-61 in July of 1956. With the arrival of the A3D Skywarrior, Savages were adapted to the aerial refueling role to support the Navy's new fuel hungry jets. (USN via Tailhook)

(Left) AJ-1 Savage of VC-8 aboard MIDWAY (CVB-41) during Midshipmen cruise in August of 1952. (D. Walsh via Bill Larkins)

COMPOSITE HEAVY ATTACK SQUADRONS

Re-designation			
Composite Squadrons Re-designated (Jul 1955)		Commissioned As Heavy Attack Squadrons	
VC-5 to VAH-5	NB	VAH-1	TB
CV-6 to VAH-6	NF	VAH-2	BF
VC-7 to VAH-7	NH	VAH-3	BW
VC-8 to VAH-8	NC	VAH-4	BI
VC-9 to VAH-9	FG	VAH-11	NG

(Below) A3D-1 (135440) of VAH-2 the second of four A3D squadrons equipped during 1956. Initially Skywarrior equipped VAH units were classified as land based mining squadrons. (MDAC via Harry Gann)

COMPOSITE EARLY WARNING SQUADRONS

The concept of carrier based *airborne early warning* (AEW) evolved during World War II when the Navy was faced with low-level attacks coming in under the shipboard radar. Postwar research and development into the AEW concept continued at San Diego, and on 6 July 1948 VAW-1 and VAW-2 were commissioned and given the responsibility of providing airborne early warning for carrier operations. A month later they were re-designated as composite squadrons, VC-11 and VC-12 respectively. Their first aircraft, which were equipped with AEW and search radar, was the Grumman TBM-3W Avenger and a few TBM-3E Avengers with special electronics. Douglas AD-3W and AD-4W Skyraiders followed in 1950, and AD-5Ws in 1953. Normally these AEW composite squadrons operated three aircraft DETs on ESSEX class carriers, and six aircraft DETs on MIDWAY class carriers. They also operated a few AD-5s, radar counter-measure AD-4Qs, and several SNB-5s for utility duties.

COMPOSITE EARLY WARNING SQUADRONS

Re-designation	
VAW-1 to VC-11 to VAW-11 ND	VAW-2 to VC-12 to VAW-12 NE

AD-4W (12771) Skyraider of VC-12 at Wayne Airport in August of 1951. The AD-4W was equipped with airborne early warning (AEW) search radar. (Roger Besecker)

COMPOSITE NIGHT ATTACK SQUADRONS

Flying TBM-3Es VC-33 was as an anti-submarine squadron when it was commissioned in May of 1949, with VC-35 following in May of 1950 in the same role. Within a year, however, sweeping changes were made when the squadrons' secondary mission of night attack was expanded when funding for sixty AD-4N night attack versions of the Skyraider was authorized during the Korean War. Other versions of the Skyraider employed were the radar countermeasure *Q* variants, and the special electronics *E* variants. A few TBM-3E and -3N Avengers remained with the squadron for a few more years. *Special weapons* AD-4Bs with the capability to deliver nuclear weapons were added in 1952, and winterized AD-4Ns were delivered under the designation AD-4NLs for operations in the cold Korean winters. Several Douglas F3D Skyknights arrived in 1951 to add jet capability to the night attack role, but the F3D was withdrawn from combat duty and used only for utility duties. By 1956 only the AD-5N remained remained in three and four aircraft night attack DETs depending upon the size of aircraft carrier they operated from. Other aircraft types used by the composite night attack squadrons included the AD-5, the radar counter measure AD-3Q, and AD-4Q, the special weapons delivery AD-6, the S2F, and the SNB.

AD-5N (122493) of VC-33 operated their Skyraiders in four plane DETs as the Fleet's primary night attack aircraft after 1955. (Duane Kasulka Collection)

TBM-3W (65840) Avenger of VC-11 flying as part of a submarine hunter-killer team with a TBM-3E of VC-25 during 1948. (USN via Clay Jansson)

(Above) AD-5 (132641) of VC-11, the squadron received its first -5s during 1953 as a utility aircraft. (Duane Kasulka Collection)

COMPOSITE NIGHT ATTACK SQUADRONS

Re-designation	
VC-33 to VA(AW)-33 SS	VC-35 to VA(AW)-35 NR

AD-1Q (09386) of VC-35 during 1949, originally in the first production batch of AD-1s, it was one of thirty-five Skyraiders modified to -1Q Electronic Counter Measure standards. (Harry Gann)

COMPOSITE NIGHT FIGHTER SQUADRONS

The role of fleet protection at night was normally handled by a pair of F6F Hellcats adapted to the night fighter role from a VF squadron teamed with a TBM Avenger from a VT squadron in the search role. With the increased post war emphasis on the night fighting role, along with new techniques in training, VC-4 was commissioned to consolidate the night protection mission. VC-4's initial aircraft included the F6F-5N, TBM-3E, -3Q, -3N, and the AD-1Q. The Martin AM-1Q Mauler was added in 1949, but lasted only a year before being phased out. VC-3 was equipped with the F4U-5N, F6F-5N, and the AD-4N which VC-4 also operated. The first jet aircraft to be used in the night fighter role was the F2H-2N Banshee which had a twenty-five inch nose extension to house radar for an all-weather capability. Initially only VC-4 operated the F2H-2N since only fourteen were built. When the F2H-2N was phased out of night fighting service several VFs used them as interim aircraft. With the outbreak of the Korean war F6F-5N Hellcats were deployed on CVE carriers, with F4U-5Ns being deployed on the larger carriers. Their primary mission was to provide all-weather fleet protection, with a secondary mission of night interdiction of enemy supply lines. Several DETs were sent ashore to eliminate North Korean *Bed Check Charlies* that were attacking Allied positions at night. By 1952 VC-3 and 4 were operating the F3D-2, the F2H-3, -2B, -2N, the F4U-5N, -5NL, plus a few F6F-5Ns which were retained until 1954 for operations from CVEs. By 1954 VC-4 was flying the F2H-4, F9F-6, F4U-5, -5N, -5NL, TV-2, and the SNB-5, while VC-3 closed out 1954 operating the F7U-3, F9F-6, FJ-3, F2H-3, F4U-5N, -5NL, TV-2, and the SNB-5. By the end of 1956 VC-3 was operating the A4D-1, the F4D-1, F3H-2N and the SNB-5. VC-4 was now operating the F9F-5, AD-5/-4W, a P2V-5, a TV-2, and a SNB-5. Normally they operated in three to seven plane DETs with the F4U and the F2H. With the arrival of all-weather jet fighters, DETs were supplied only to the smaller carriers. By 1956 VC-3 flying the AD-5 and for utility duties used the F9F-5, AD-4Q, PV-5, TV-2, and SNB, while VC-4 operated the F3H-2N, the F4D-1, A4D-1, and the SNB.

COMPOSITE NIGHT FIGHTER SQUADRONS

Re-designation	
VC-3 to VF(AW)-3 NP	VC-4 to VF(AW)-4 NA

F4U-5N (124713) Corsair nightfighter of VC-3 trimmed in Red, outlined in White at Moffett Field in May of 1954. The Corsair remained operational with VC-3 until late 1955. (Bill Larkins Collection)

(Below) F3D-2 (124833) of VC-4 which operated a few Skyknights throughout 1953 as a jet training aircraft. (Clay Jansson)

(Above) F3H-2N (133581) Demon of VFAW-3 at Oakland in July of 1956. In addition to providing all-weather DETs to the Fleet, VFAW-3 also evaluated new jet aircraft during this time. (Bill Larkins)

(Below) F4D-1 (134780) Skyray carrying its new VFAW-3 designation on its fin fillet at Alameda during July of 1956. (Lional Paul Collection)

(Above) F2H-2N (123307) Banshee of VC-3, this night fighter version of the Banshee was flown operationally only by VC-4. (Pete Bowers)

COMPOSITE PHOTOGRAPHIC SQUADRONS

Carrier based aerial reconnaissance was formally added to the fleet in January of 1949 with the commissioning of VC-61 and VC-62. The importance of the reconnaissance role was obvious when it was established that eighty-five per cent of all information gathered against the Axis powers during World War II had been through aerial reconnaissance, and this approached ninety-five per cent during the Korean war. Initially these composite photographic squadrons were equipped with the F6F-5P and F8F-2P, and later with the F4U-4P and F4U-5P. During 1951 the first jets arrived as the F9F-2P Panther went into service, and in 1952 the F2H-2P and the F9F-5P went into service. The prop driven Corsair was phased out the same year, and the swept wing F9F-6P Cougar was introduced in 1953 augmenting the F2H-2Ps. The F9F-8P was added in late 1955. Initially two aircraft DETs were deployed, but this was increased to three aircraft with the arrival of jets and larger carriers. A variety of support aircraft were also operated which included the F9F-6, SNJ-4, F2H-2, F7U-3P, TV-2, and SNB-5P.

COMPOSITE PHOTOGRAPHIC SQUADRONS

Re-designation	
VC-61 to VFP-61 PP	VC-62 to VFP-62 TL* to PL *Used initially but changed prior to 1958.

F8F-2P (121760) Bearcat of VC-62 painted with war game White stripes flying from MIDWAY (CVB-41) in January of 1951. (USN/NA)

(Below) F8F-2P (121735) Bearcat of VC-62. This squadron was commissioned in January of 1949 being assigned the TL tail code, but was changed to TP during April of 1950. (Lional Paul Collection)

(Below) F9F-5Ps of VC-61 flying from BOXER (CV-21) in 1953. (Grumman Aerospace Corp)

(Below) F9F-6P (134460) Cougar of VC-61 at Miramar during 1955. The photo Cougar entered Fleet service in 1956. (Bill Larkins)

(Above) F9F-8P (141700) photo Cougar of VC-61 at Mines Field in June of 1956. Typical DETs were three aircraft. (Bill Larkins Collection)

(Right) F2H-2P Banshees of VC-62 carrying CVG-17's tail code and 900 series aircraft numbers flying by Mount Fuji in December of 1953. (USN)

(Below) F2H-2P (126681) Banshee of VFP-61 at Miramar in the new Light Gray over White aircraft schemes, and the new squadron designation assigned in July of 1956. (Roger Besecker)

HEAVY PHOTOGRAPHIC SQUADRONS

The Navy's long range aerial reconnaissance squadrons (VP) had been closed out with the decommissioning of land based VP-61 and VP-62 in January of 1950. This role was re-established with the commissioning of VJ-61 and VJ-62 to provide the fleet with long range photographic capability and the ability to operate from carriers. This role of carrier based long range aerial reconnaissance was considered so critical that the first eighteen North American AJ-2 Savages were modified for the long range reconnaissance role under the designation AJ-2P. The reconnaissance AJ-2P Savage operated from MIDWAY and ESSEX class carriers in DETs of one to three aircraft. Additional aircraft used for training and support functions included the P4Y-1P, SNB-5, -5P, P2V-3W and AJ-2.

VJ-61 and VJ-62 were re-designated VAP-61 and VAP-62.

HEAVY PHOTOGRAPHIC SQUADRONS

Re-designation	
VJ-61 to VAP-61 PB	VJ-62 to VAP-62 TP

AJ-2P of VJ-62 at Norfolk, provided long range photographic coverage in one to three aircraft DETs. (USN via Clay Jansson)

(Below) AJ-2P (129185) Savage of VJ-61 at Oakland during 1954 warming for takeoff. Red trim is on the nose radome and top of the vertical fin. (Gordon Williams)

CARRIER
ANTI-SUBMARINE
SQUADRONS

Formal anti-submarine warfare (ASW) began with the commissioning of CVEG-1 and CVEG-2 in 1946. These CVE air groups operated a fighter and attack squadron plus a DET from an early warning composite squadron. Initially one of the fighter squadrons was equipped with Ryan FR-1 Fireballs which were later replaced by the F6F-5 and -5N Hellcats that already equipped the other squadrons. The attack squadrons operated the TBM-3E Avenger in the search role, while early warning VC DETs operated the TBM-3W Avenger. On 15 September 1948 CVEG-1, 2 and 3 were redesignated anti-submarine composite squadrons VC-21, VC-22 and VC-23, with their F6F-5N Hellcats being reassigned to squadrons designated composite night squadrons (VCNs). At this same time composite ASW squadron VC-31, was commissioned. These new anti-submarine warfare composite squadrons continued to operate TBM-3E and TBM-3S Avengers in the attack role, and the TBM-3W in the search role. During April of 1950 those VC squadrons involved in the carrier based ASW role were redesignated carrier anti-submarine squadrons (VSs).

The new Grumman AF-2S and AF-2W Guardian, which first entered fleet service with VS-25 in October of 1950, began to replace the TBM Avengers. The AF Guardian was the first ASW designed aircraft for carrier aviation. The AF-2S performed the attack role while the AF-2W performed the search role. During the Korean War six reserve ASW squadrons were activated and re-designated fleet units in 1953. The prospect of a much enlarged Soviet submarine force, and the lessons learned during the Korean War, led the Navy to further expand the VAW squadrons and CVS force, and by 1952 there were fifteen anti-submarine squadrons with ten operating the AF Guardian and five the TBM Avenger. The AF-3S Guardian that came into service carried additional submarine detection gear. Escort carriers (CVEs) which had ASW squadrons aboard were redesignated anti-submarine warfare carriers (CVSs in 1953 along with those CVAs which had not been upgraded to operate jets.

In February of 1954 the twin engine Grumman S2F-1 Tracker, which combined in a single aircraft both the search and attack roles, joined the fleet with VS-26. By 1956 all squadrons were converted, or were in the process of converting to the S2F Tracker, with each being assigned a utility SNB-5 while shore based. Each squadron normally carried twenty aircraft on strength.

(Above) TBM-3S (91152) Avenger of VS-21 flying near San Diego in June of 1950. (USN)

(Below) TBM-3E Avengers of reserve VS-892 originally from Seattle, and activated during the Korean War. Point Loma, February of 1951. (Tailhook)

(Above) TBM-3E (81532) Avenger of VS-23, only one other VS squadron had tail codes that did not begin with an S, San Diego in December of 1951. (USN)

(Below) TBM-3W (69476) Avenger of VS-32 aboard PALAU (CVE-122) awaiting launch in July of 1951. (Pete Bowers Collection)

(Above) AF-2W (130395) of VS-37 flown by Ensign Mentges in March of 1955 off the coast of Japan. Trim colors are white. (USN)

(Above) AF-2S and AF-2W Guardian ASW hunter-killer teams of reserve VS-801 in October of 1952. VS-801 was re-designated Fleet VS-30 in 1953. (USN/NA via Jim Sullivan)

(Below) S2F-1 (136398) of VS-20. Originally a reserve unit from Willow Grove (VS-931), it was retained in the Fleet to boost ASW capability. (Bill Larkins)

(Above) S2F-1 (136482) of VS-36 preparing to take off from Oklahoma City during September of 1956 in its new Light Gray over White color scheme. ASW rockets and a depth charge are carried on the port underwing. (Gordon Williams)

(Below) S2F-1 (133073) of VS-26 accelerating during its launch from ANTIETAM (CVS-36) in late 1954. VS-26 was the first squadron to operate the Tracker. (Grumman Aerospace Corp)

CARRIER ANTI-SUBMARINE SQUADRONS

Initial Composite and Re-designation (April 1950)		Korean War Reserve Call-up and Re-designation to Fleet Anti-Submarine Squadrons		
VC-21 to VS-21	BS	**Reserve Station**		
VC-22 to VS-22*	SL	Miami	VS-801 to VS-30	SW
VC-23 to VS-23	MI	New York	VS-831 to VS-36	SD
VC-31 to VS-31	SP	Oakland	VS-871 to VS-37	SU
Commissioned As Carrier Anti-Submarine Squadrons		Seattle	VS-892 to VS-38	ST
		Squantum	VS-913 to VS-39	SN
		Willow Grove	VS-931 to VS-20*	SV
VS-24*	SI			
VS-25*	SK	*Decommissioned prior to July 1956.*		
VS-26*	SH			
VS-27	SM			
VS-32	SR			

HELICOPTER ANTI-SUBMARINE SQUADRONS

The first helicopter anti-submarine warfare squadron, HS-1, was commissioned on 3 October 1951 at NAS Key West. Initially equipped with the interim Piasecki HUP-1 helicopter, they received the improved HUP-2 in April of the following year. Two months later HS-1 began *quals* aboard the escort carrier SIBONEY. The HUP-2 was considered unsuitable for aircraft carrier ASW operations but continued in this role under the designation HUP-2S while a suitable replacement was being developed. HS-2 received the Sikorsky HO4S, a helicopter built especially for the ASW role, but the new helicopter was quickly found to fall short of expectations. It would be 1955 before a truly operational ASW helicopter, the Sikorsky HSS-1, would join the Fleet having both the search and attack capability. In the interim the HO4S helicopter was modified to the HO4S-3, and HO4S-3S for operational ASW squadron use in two and four helicopter DETs. Additional squadrons were added as HSS-1 and HSS-1N helicopters became available until there was a squadron available for each CVS carrier. The HSS-1N was capable of both day and night operations and had automatic hovering capability. The Bell HTL-3 and the Beech JRB-4 were employed by the squadrons as training aircraft.

HELICOPTER ANTI-SUBMARINE SQUADRONS

HS-1	HU	HS-4	VO	HS-7	PS
HS-2	HV	HS-5	HY	HS-8	PJ
HS-3	HW	HS-6	PF	HS-9	HJ

Piasecki HUP-2S (128572) of HS-3. The HUP-2 joined the HS community in April of 1952, with a number being modified for ASW duties under the designation HUP-2S. (USN/NA)

(Below) HSS-1 (139021) of HS-1, the Navy's first truly operational ASW helicopter was introduced to the Fleet in 1956. Oklahoma City in September of 1956. (Gordon Williams)

HELICOPTER UTILITY SQUADRONS

The helicopter, under evaluation by Operational Development Squadron Three (VX-3) for the search and rescue (SAR) role passed from an experimental status to the utility status on 1 April 1948 when HU-1s and HU-2s were commissioned at Lakehurst along with the Sikorsky HO3S-1 and the Bell HTL-2. HU-1s were assigned to the West Coast, and HU-2s remained to support the East Coast Fleet. During the summer of 1948 the squadrons began providing two helicopter DETs to fleet carriers as plane guards, the first ones being assigned aboard BOXER and PRINCETON. Most of these early assignments were the four place HO3S-1 helicopter. This was followed by the HO4S in 1950, and the Piasecki HUP in 1951, which served out this time period supplying two helicopter DETs. Other types of helicopters included the HTL-4, and -5, HUP-2, and -2S, HRS-2, and several fixed wing utility aircraft such as the SNJ and SBD.

(Below) HUP-2 (128519) of HU-2 carrying a large penguin insignia with a telescope tucked under its flipper, and powered by rotors on the helmet and tail. Philadelphia in September of 1955. (Bill Steeneck via Bill Larkins)

HELICOPTER UTILITY SQUADRONS

HU-1 UP	HU-2 UR

(Left) This HO3S-1 of HU-1 is lifting off the flight deck to take up a station aft of the carrier to serve as a plane guard during flight operations. (USN/NA via Stan Piet)